Lace

by L. W. van der Meulen-Nulle

UNIVERSE BOOKS Inc.
381 PARK AVENUE SOUTH
NEW YORK 16, NEW YORK

The original edition of this book was published in
The Netherlands by C. A. J. van Dishoeck - Bussum
Cover: Detail of Priest's Alb. Needlepoint Lace

First Printing

Published in the United States of America by

UNIVERSE BOOKS, Inc.

381 Park Avenue South

New York 16, New York

Library of Congress Catalog Card Number: 64-10343

Copyright in The Netherlands 1964 by C. A. J. van Dishoeck - Bussum

Printed in The Netherlands.

Foreword

The object of this book is to give a general impression of the design and technical finish of the different kinds of lace, illustrated by a careful selection of Plates.

I have explained in detail the technical differences in the art of lace work, so that the reader will be able to understand and distinguish the different methods used. The book is not only meant for people who wish to know more about these laces, but I hope it will also be used in schools, so that students will know the history of hand-worked lace, before the use of machine-made lace, and so appreciate the artistry of these hand-made laces.

The society 'Het Kantsalet' of Holland, helped to edit this book and to collect the plates. H. M. Queen Juliana has given her permission for the reproduction of a painting belonging to the Royal Family, and I wish to thank the many museums and some private persons who have given their permission for reproductions of paintings in this book.

L. W. van der Meulen-Nulle.

I What is Lace?

Lace is a weave made entirely by the lace-worker. Close and open mesh-work interchanges in a greater or lesser degree, giving the lace a heavy or a fine appearance. In making lace the worker does not first take a piece of material to work on, but creates the weave with one or many threads. All openwork weaves that are crocheted, knitted or knotted including tatting which is worked with a spool, are lace products.

Needlepoint lace

To make needlepoint lace a pattern is drawn on parchment or dark paper; this drawing is sewn on to double linen which makes it easier to separate later on. Two threads are sewn along the edges of the ornament to attach the rows of stitches of flowers and leaves and such motifs as well as ornamental stitches and background. When the lace is finished, the stitches fastening the outlining cord to the linen are cut away thus releasing the finished lace.

Bobbin lace

Bobbin lace is the fairy-like weave made with either silver, gold, linen, cotton, silk or wool thread, which is wound on bobbins. The drawing is attached to the pillow or cushion and the pins are then stuck through the drawing with the pillow, leaving half of each pin standing clear and forming the *framework* round which the thread is built up into lace. Each pin remains in its place until a section of the pattern is completed, when the back pins are removed and replaced into the repeat part of the design so that the continuity is maintained.

II Origin of Lace

The source of lace is not known, but needle lace was originally practised most in Italy and Flanders so either country
could claim the distinction of introducing lace.
We can tell from paintings that both bobbin and needlepoint
lace started about 1500.
Openwork weaves have been found in the sarcophagi of
ancient Egypt.
In the Orient, the cradle of many of our industries, light
weaves such as gauze and muslin were used for voiles and
veils. Sometimes a few threads were pulled out and they were
then decorated with embroidery and trimmings were plaited
and finished with knotted fringes — a similar decoration to
that used by the ancient Romans.
Needlepoint lace as we know it, must have developed from
embroidery, while the knotting of trimmings was the fore-
runner of bobbin lace.

Holbeinstitch

When linen began to be used in the fifteenth century for
outer clothing, new opportunities for adornment introduced
the working of coloured thread, such as can be seen in con-
temporary paintings of the period, notably Holbein and

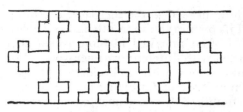

Holbein pattern

7

Dürer, and the decoration portrayed either on sleeves or neckline looked most attractive on the usually dark clothing of that time.

Pattern books of the sixteenth century give many examples of this work, and in the Boymans-Van Beuningen Museum in Rotterdam there is a painting by Pieter Aertsen called 'Pancake Bakery' (1560) which shows the beauty of these trimmings.

The decoration made with this stitch is so rich and varied that it was taught again in the nineteenth century under the name of 'Holbeinstitch'.

Fringe

In the sixteenth century cloths were also woven from which the shearing threads on both sides were plaited as a fringe.

Macramé

The macramé method practised in the sixteenth and seventeenth century, especially in Italy, is most probably Arabian in origin. The lace products made in this knotting technique were used principally for embellishing furniture, with its large distinctive patterns where the human figure is often cleverly portrayed in the squares. In the illustrated work 'Die Sammlung Ikle' three beautiful specimens are reproduced.

Filet

The knotting of fishing net led to the filet lace, a technique which not only held its own in the sixteenth and seventeenth century but was also often practised in more recent times. Knotted squares darned with different ornaments were worked into spreads and covers with embroidery. According to E. Lefébure 'in the estate of Catherine de Medici many such squares were found. 381 unornamented squares and 538 squares decorated with roses and bouquets are reported'. Filets were also knotted large enough to be made into covers from one piece; in that case the drawing covered the whole

1. Decoration of a shirt (1529). 2. Reticella lace, geometrical ornament in two designs. (Late 16th or early 17th century.) 3. Filet guipure with bobbin lace edge.

4. *Millstone collar, cuffs and cap with Italian bobbin lace (Beatrix van Sypesteyn 1593—1663).*

5. *Venetian lady with Medicis or Stuart collar, cuffs, dress flounces and handkerchief with Italian needlepoint lace.*

6. *Cap, collar, cuffs and apron with bobbin lace.* **D. D. Santvoort** *(1610—1680).*

7. *Millstone collar, so-called Fraises, Italian bobbin lace. 8. Flemish lace pillow on a painting by Brekelenkam (1620—1668).*

9. Standing up collar and cuffs of *Reticella* lace (1620).

10. *Alb with flounce, insertions and cuffs of Venetian needlepoint laçe.*

11. Jabot, the so-called Steenkerkentie and cuffs of Venetian needlepoint lace (1680).

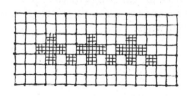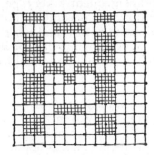

Filet pattern

network and was either a religious or a mythological scene. Sometimes there was a separate centre-piece surrounded by edging in which there was a more realistic picture.

The Rijksmuseum (Amsterdam) possesses a cloth (Plate 3) in filet technique with nine knotted squares, together forming one beautiful design. In the large centre-square are the arms of two Dutch families: to the left Sickinghe, to the right Jongema. The cloth is signed by the worker with the initials O.V.S. and so we presume that this is worked by a 'Sickinghe'. It is dated 1623. The whole cloth is surrounded by fine pointed bobbin lace, possibly Italian work. Probably this filet cloth served as an ornament or cover. The Rijksmuseum also has in its possession a cover, composed from 156 squares worked in different techniques, namely filet, bobbin lace and embroidery, and surrounded by a Flemish bobbin lace. Four filet squares have a coat of arms ornament, two with the name Pieck, one with the name Poll (dated 1623), and the other with the name Balnerin.

These squares, interesting because of the date, the arms and the names, are placed completely at random in between the other squares.

Fils tirés (Pulled and drawn threads)

The fils tirés is the most elaborate of linen decoration and was consequently very popular in the colourful sixteenth century, for decorating not only collars and cuffs, but also children's aprons and table cloths, as paintings of that period show. It is used to-day for shawls, altars, and tablecloths. The ornament could arise in different ways:

1. By drawing together the threads of the background, using a loosely woven linen through which the sewing together of the threads was simple. For simplicity a single thread was sometimes taken out at regular intervals. The background was sewn together with red, blue, black or yellow threads. This is known as 'pulled' or Dresden work as opposed to that technically known as 'drawn thread' work.

2. By open working of the background. A certain number of the threads of the linen part, meant for background, were taken out at regular intervals in length and width. The threads that were left over were sewn together with white thread to give the impression of a network of squares.

3. By taking out the threads of the whole part to be decorated at regular intervals and by sewing the threads left between the openings into a network of squares. The flowers, leaves, animal-forms etc. were effected by filling in the squares with ornamental stitches.

4. By taking out the threads of the whole of the ornamental part and sewing together the remaining threads for the background of the ornament, into a network of small squares and by filling in with a thicker thread where the pulled out parts of the pattern are going to be.

The Rijksmuseum in Amsterdam owns a sheet of this work, a magnificent example, with hare and trees succeeding each other. The Boymans-Van Beuningen Museum in Rotterdam also owns such a sheet of the seventeenth century but with a different design.

Quintin or Buratto

It was found that the pulling out of threads took a lot of time, and a material was produced already open-worked with squares. According to E. Lefébure this material was made in Brittany where it was called 'Quintin' and in Italy a similar weave was called 'Buratto'.

The special distinguishing mark of this weave is that length and width differ in thickness; one way had one single thread, the other way two threads repeatedly twisted round each other. The motif was usually stopped in one direction, namely in the direction of the length of the drawing. The Buratto weave is still made in Italy.

Lacis

In France Quintin material was also called 'Lacis'. As this work served not only for religious purposes but also as an ornament for furniture, it existed in many colours, as well as in white.

Point Coupé

The immediate predecessor of needlepoint lace was the Point Coupé. This was openwork embroidery in which at first small parts of the material were cut out, square, round, rectangular or any other shape and the apertures were filled in with ornamental stitches. A good example of this can be seen in the Boymans-Van Beuningen Museum in the painting of Jacob Willemsz., Delft, dated 1592. The woman, Baertje van Adrichem, pictured on this painting wears a pair of cuffs in Point Coupé; they are embroidered, have already fils-tirés edges as well as round cut-out apertures, filled in with ornamental stitches. When there was enough room, some threads of the weave were left in the aperture, stretched as diagonal threads, and these as bases making possible the working of a richer ornament. To prevent fraying along the cut-out material the surroundings of the hole were bound with a buttonhole stitch as shown on Plate 2. Around bigger

11

square or rectangular apertures some edges were worked while the threads were pulled together, forming in this way a fils-tirés frame. The threads of the linen left over in the hole, as well as those sewn in diagonal lines were woven in pairs, like figures of eight, to form bars connecting two parts of the lace motifs, the so called 'point de reprise'. The rest of the ornament was not only defined by the size of the aperture but also by the left over weave threads and the diagonally stretched threads. That is why it was a geometrical composition when it was first practised, with a triangular, square or tape form, but later on it became more elaborate, and the spaces were filled with human and animal figures or a floral ornament; the preparation of an aperture in linen for this treatment was meticulous and slow, but as soon as it was known that the larger aperture could be divided by stretching the threads, then it was realised that the outline could be formed the same way. This meant that it was no longer thought necessary to adhere to a definite form in the linen, and so lace was born.

Point coupé pattern

Pattern Books

Although made throughout Europe, the Point Coupé probably started in Italy. At first, the drawn patterns were passed from hand to hand; but with the invention of engraving and the art of printing in the fifteenth century their popularity spread. Good models were much in demand and so the printing and editing of pattern books increased. The first known pattern book was issued in 1527 with the title 'Livre nouveau et subtil touchant l'art et science tant de broderie, fronssures, tapisserie, comme autres métiers qu'on fait à l'aiguille', and was designed by Pierre Quinty from Cologne.

The second edition was in German and was signed Quintell. This book consists only of patterns for lacis but not yet for laces ('L'Histoire de la dentelle' by Mme Bury-Palisser). E. Lefébure writes about this in detail in 'Broderie et Dentelles', from which the following is taken: 'Several pattern books followed, in which lace was mentioned, among others those in 1528 by Antonio Tagliente and in 1530 by Nicole d'Aristotile'. Tagliente called his first book 'Esempio di ricami'. In the text he said that the design could be carried out in linen, silk, gold and silver and he produced the drawings in order of technical skill, of which the last one was called 'Punto in aere' (Point en l'air — lace without background of linen). In Italy 'Punto in aere' is the general name for needlepoint lace.

In 1543 Rob. Mathio Pagan edited in Venice his first pattern book which was devoted to 'Point Coupé and Broderie sur toile claire', and in a later edition in 1558 he published for the first time patterns for needlepoint lace. In 1584 the Italian Dominique de Sera edited in Paris a book called 'Livre de lingerie, enseignant le noble et gentil art de l'esquille'. In it he described what he had seen in Italy, Spain, Rumania, Germany and other countries, but since he was most probably afraid that it would not be enough for his French clients, he added: 'divers patrons de l'invention de Jean Cousin, peintre à Paris'. In 1594 there appeared in Venice a pattern book written by Madame Isabella Cantanea Parasole called: 'Specchio delle virtuose done' (Mirror for virtuous women); this book contained patterns for needlepoint and bobbin lace and from the accuracy of the drawing it can be concluded that she must have been an able worker herself, or that she was at least well acquainted with the techniques. The following year an edition appeared in Rome.

Drawings of Italian origin were usually formed of rosettes, garlands and conventional leaves. The open space was divided into partitions by columns, vases and fountains. Figures of

Saints interchanged with the Gods of the Olympus, while fauns, nymphs, and musical instruments were also frequently used and in some ornaments the Arabian influence could definitely be seen. In drawings of French or German origin however, the whole design was naturalistic.

Because patterns of different origin were published in these books, it appears that the editors were not always the designers, but that they had collected for their books patterns originating in different countries. Of these patternbooks a few are left. Several of them were reprinted in 1883 in Paris by Amand-Durand called 'Livres à dentelles'. Six parts of these are in the Rijksprentenkabinet in Amsterdam.

III The Use of Laces

It would not be possible to write a book about lace without
mentioning its many uses. Lace appears on clothing and
about the home around 1500. The clothes of both adults and
children were of an extraordinary magnificence, being made
of beautiful materials with luxurious finery. Part of this
finery was the decoration of linen that was then used extensively on outer clothing. Linen trimming developed into small
wavy collars or ruffs, and cuffs, out of which grew the wavy
collar and wide cuff, bordered with lace.

Fraises

According to Quicherat 'Histoire du costume en France' in
1540 collars were already part of the man's costume and they
were called 'collerettes à fraises' (Plate 4). They enclosed the
neck, were starched and kept in shape with laiton. As the
collars became larger and standing away more from the neck,
they became less comfortable to wear. These are the so called
'millstone collars' on which up to 17 yards of a fine or coarse
linen was trimmed with lace. Apart from beautiful collars
and cuffs on their dresses women mostly were pictured hold-
ing a handkerchief bordered with lace (Plate 5). The painting of the Infanta Isabella in the Brussels Museum shows the
high standards of luxury and the beautiful laces that were
then being made.
On the portrait painted by J. R. van Ravesteyn (in the
Mauritshuis in the Hague), Ernestine Jolande, wife of Graaf
Johann van Nassau-Siegen wears a beautiful wavy collar
decorated with bobbin lace.

Seventeenth Century

The costume of Beatrix van Sypesteyn 1593—1663 (Sypesteyn
Museum in Loosdrecht) has, in addition to the beautiful
fraise collar, worked with bobbin lace, pretty cuffs and a cap,
bordered with lace of a different design from the collar. The

15

spotless white decoration of linen and lace with this dark toilet gives it a quiet distinction and elegance (Plate 4).

The end of the sixteenth century brings a change in the lace ornamentation of the costume. Some gentlemen now wear the collars that were so uncomfortable before, without starch and laiton, so that they lie flat on the costume. Van Dyck painted the Mayor of Antwerp with such a collar (collection Hanfstaengl in Munich Kgl. Pinakothek). A number of participants at the 'Dinner of Officers of the Cloveniersdoelen' (Frans Hals, 1627) also wear turned-down pleated collars (Frans Hals Museum, Haarlem).

Medicis or Stuart collar

Women's collars adopted an opening in the front, to begin with still pleated, but later on standing straight up against the hair; the so-called Medicis or Stuart collar (Plate 5). In the Mauritshuis in the Hague there are pictured in the painting by Frans Francken d.J. and Frans Pourbus d.J. 'Ball at the Court of Albertus of Austria and his wife Isabella' some women with pleated and smooth Stuart collars, while a man's costume shows already a bulging flat collar.

The portrait of a man painted by Salomon Mesdach (1620; Rijksmuseum), shows him in his beautiful early seventeenth century costume with an extraordinarily shaped collar (Plate 9).

Understandably, washing these collars was time-wasting and difficult work. Many men insisted on starching their own collar, including Henry III (Die Mode). Max von Boehm also tells us:

Italian bobbin lace

16

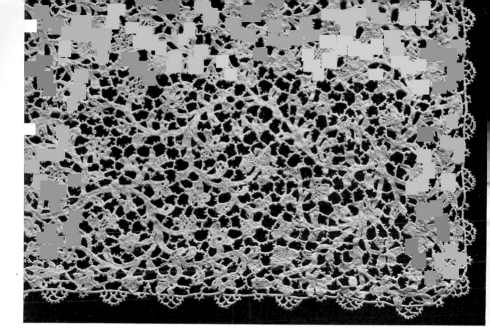

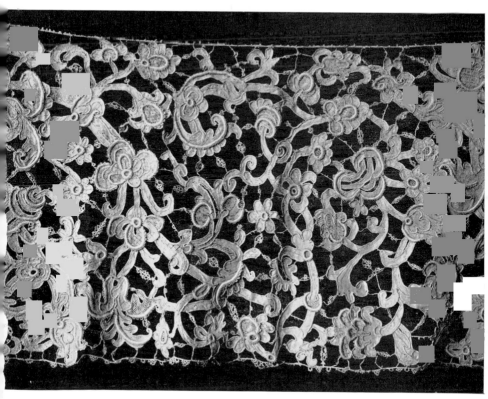

12. Part of jabot of Italian needlepoint lace (1680). 13. Flounce of Italian needlepoint lace. Venise à gros relief (second half 17th century).

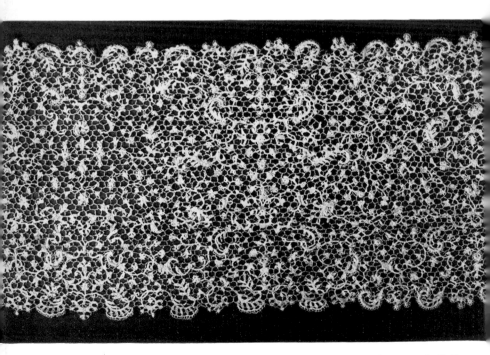

14. Dress attire, Point de France needlepoint lace (second half 17th century). Coiffure: Appliqué de Bruxelles, bobbin lace on tulle. H.M. the Queen Mother of Holland (1933). 15. Coiffure à la Fontange, dress attire and sleeve flounces Point de France. Queen Mary Stuart (1662—1692). 16. Flounce Point de France, needlepoint lace. (Late 17th century, or early 18th century).

17. Jabot, Point de France needlepoint lace (1697).

18. *Vest with frill and sleeve flounces of Point d'Alençon needlepoint lace.*

'That a certain Mrs. Turner had invented a starch, that coloured yellow instead of blue. The different parties in England made known their political disposition through their collar. A blue-starched collar meant that one was disposed towards the Catholic faith, and a yellow-starched collar was worn by people sympathetic to the Huguenots'.

Turn-down collar

Around 1620 the form of the collar changed, and became on the ladies' costume a turn-down one, sometimes consisting of two or three layers on top of each other and continuing along the décolleté, or the linen frontpiece covering the décolleté, and finished off with a lace edging. A cap, also with a lace edging, completed the costume. The portrait of Agathe Geelvinck, wife of Frederik Dircksz. Alewijn, painted by Santvoort (1639), shows a beautiful collar with a double folded wrap; the edging is finished off with the most luxurious Flemish bobbin lace (Plate 26).

The child's portrait (Plate 6), painted by Dirck Dircksz. Santvoort, shows the elegance of the child's costume. Collar, cuffs, apron and dress are decorated with the same lace, and the feathered cap has a wide piece circling the face. Several yards of lace are used for this costume. The beautiful chain over the right shoulder holds the rattle, one of the elaborate children's playthings of the day, some examples of which can still be seen.

The luxury of the ladies' costume had assumed enormous proportions. Apart from expensive collars, pearls and jewellery were in great demand.

'For a thanksgiving service on the 24th November, 1588 (Defeat of the Armada), Queen Elizabeth had a dress made, completely covered with jewels. When she died she left three thousand expensive dresses and it is said that members of the English parliament told the new Queen Anne of Scotland that she must wear these dresses and to purchase only the most necessary new toilets' (Die Mode). 'On 14th September 1606 at the Christening of Louis XIII,

17

Maria de Medici wore a dress covered with 32000 pearls and 3000 diamonds' (Die Mode).

The men's costumes were finished off with a pair of cuffs and a collar, which fell, either cut square or round, over the back and shoulders and was fastened in front with a cord, on which were tassels (Plate 28). Not only on the collars and cuffs was lace worn but it was also used on other garments.

'In the inventory of the Earl of Rutland there were among others nineteen shirts trimmed with lace. Charles I of England bought once a hundred yards of lace as trimming for twelve shirts and more than six hundred yards for his nightshirts. In 1638 in England three to four pounds was spent on simple men's collars, but Louis XIV had collars that cost 250 écus d'or'.

At first collars for both men and women were alike.

'So it was counted as a courtesy when Gustaaf Adolf at the ball that the city of Augsburg gave in his honour in 1642, took off his collar and offered it to Miss Jacobine Lauber, as belle of the ball' (Die Mode, Max von Boehm).

In the collection at the Rijksmuseum are two shirts finished off with such lace flounces, worn by Casimir I and a shirt with a lace collar that belonged to Stadtholder William III.

These different collars, namely the fraises, the Medicis, the half-turn-down and the turn-down ones were worn simultaneously in the seventeenth century. In the painting on which the family of the Mayor, Dr. Dirck Bas Jacobsz. is immortalized, the parents wear the sixteenth century model and the eldest children the still standing-back collar, whereas the younger daughter has the turn-down collar on her dress (D. D. Santvoort, 1634, Rijksmuseum).

Canons

As well as collars and cuffs in the men's costume lace was used round the knees and in riding boots. Lace knee flounces were called 'Canons', in France. 'At the French Court one could pay 13000 thaler for a trimming, consisting of collar, cuffs and canons. Cinq Mars, favourite of Louis XIII was beheaded in 1642 and left three hundred pairs of trimmings for riding boots' (Die Mode), and as many collars and pairs of cuffs (Lefébure). The low shoes were set with lace rosettes, and were also rather expensive. 'In England the price varied between thirty shillings and five pounds, but particularly fine rosettes were as much as thirty pounds a pair'. Needlepoint and bobbin lace were the most in demand and paintings show splendidly reproduced products of Italian and Venetian industrial art. The floral design became popular and the drawing of each repeat was symmetrical and stylized. In 1625 the repeat was still rather sharp and pointed (Plates 4, 5, 6, 7 and 9), but by 1640 a rounder edged repeat is used (Plate 26) (Rembrandt's paintings). The lace, with this design, added greatly to the distinction and charm of the costume.

Prohibitions and Regulations

Regulations and laws were made to try to curb the extravagant tastes of the aristocracy which was ruining itself in its efforts to wear the most beautiful clothes, in which lace, either of linen, gold or silver thread played the most important part. During the prohibition of 1623 a small smooth collar became the fashion, in Spain called the 'Golilla' collar. This had originally served as undercollar, on top of which the large millstone collar rested. The prohibition was so enforced, that when Charles I came to Madrid to ask for the hand of the Infanta Maria, he had first to take off his lace collar and put on a golilla, before he was allowed to enter the Spanish Court balls (Die Mode). Small collars also became fashionable in the Netherlands, as painted so often by the Dutch and Flemish masters. Members of the civil guard at dinner immortalized by Van der Helst in 1648 wear this model with or without lace (Rijksmuseum).
In Italy the extravagant use of lace was already controlled in 1514. One of the articles forbade young people to wear lace before their twenty-fifth birthday, with a fine of two hundred ducats, although on special occasions dispensation was given, for example in 1574 at the visit of Henry III.

There were also prohibitions in France, especially under Louis XIII, the first of which dates from 1629, called 'Regulations on excess of clothing'. This prohibition was broken several times and was not taken seriously. There are some amusing engravings by Abraham Bosse criticising the prohibition. In 1660 before the marriage of Louis XIV with the Infanta Maria of Spain, a prohibition was issued controlling the use of galloons, guipures and fine laces. Molière composed the following poem on it:

'Oh! trois et quatre fois bénit soit cet édit
Par qui des vêtements le luxe est interdit!
Les peines des maris ne seront plus si grandes
Et les femmes auront un frein à leurs demandes.
Oh! que je sais au roi bon gré de ces décris,
Et que, pour le repos de ces mêmes maris,
Je voudrais bien qu'on fit de la coquetterie
Comme de la guipure et de la broderie'.

In 1660 there also appeared an anonymous satire, called 'La révolte des passements'; this was ascribed to Mademoiselle la Trousse, a niece of Madame de Sévigné. This satire is of importance in the history of lace, as it names the different laces of the time, including one of which we know nothing to-day, namely the Point de Raguse, which probably belonged to the fine Venetian needlepoint laces. (See pages 207—209 'Broderie et Dentelles', Lefébure.)

The Elector Maximilian of Bavaria issued a decree in 1626 on the types of clothing allowed for each of the seven classes. Lace was also used for decorating furniture. According to Lefébure, in the inventory of Charles de Bourbon and his wife, the Countess of Soissons, a whole bed ornament was included with the description that the lace was put on the tester, around the columns of the bed and on the 'parade spread'. That lace was used extensively for bedroom decoration is fully confirmed by the magnificent spread, shown in the Rijksmuseum, dated 1635, and the footcover (Plate 3).

20

Col rabat

A new type of collar for the men's costume appeared in the second half of the seventeenth century. The adoption of the long wig, which hung down the back, was responsible as the collar then became short in the back with an edging of lace about four inches wide. In front the linen was brought back to a very small piece, while the lace, fastened on it, consisted of two square cornered pieces, forming together a symmetrical drawing; these frontpieces were all in one piece with the back. The collar was tied up with two cords, on which there were tassels, and was given the name of col rabat (Plate 28). Beautiful collars of Italian and French needlepoint lace have been handed down. The Rijksmuseum in Amsterdam owns two particularly pretty examples, one of which is on loan. The Cluny Museum in Paris and the Victoria & Albert Museum in London each exhibit a col rabat, with a more intricate design than the one in Amsterdam. The Willet Holthuysen Museum, also in Amsterdam, has in its collection a similar Venetian collar (Point de Venise), of which the display of lines is finer than that of the one in the Rijksmuseum but the design is not so attractive.

The self-portrait of the painter G. Terborch in the Maurits-huis in The Hague shows him, with a beautiful needlepoint lace col rabat, while the paintings of Aert van Nes and his wife Geertruida den Dubbelde painted by Bartholomeus van der Helst show how lavish the gold and black laces were, thus making the clothing so much more attractive (Plate 28, gold laces).

Cravat or Jabot and Steenkerkentie

The col rabat was followed by the cravat (Jabot), which had a long popularity on men's costumes in particular (Plate 12). This was fastened under the chin in different ways. Many paintings show us a double or triple bow, over which hangs the pleated lace in the centre, but as Plate 11 shows, Engel de Ruyter, son of Admiral Michiel de Ruyter wears a linen tie fastened round his neck, the ends finished off with a lace

21

edging. After 1692 this tie was called Cravate à la Steen-kerken.

Lace worn on armour is not unusual as the paintings in our Museums show.

Ladies' round collar. Fontange coiffure

In the middle of the seventeenth century a round collar was introduced on the décolleté of the ladies tightly enclosing the shoulders and also a collar encircling the neck. A beautiful example of this is in Plate 27. Many of these collars were made in this Flemish bobbin lace technique in which the background and the ornament were worked at the same time. If a broad collar was required (Plate 27, portrait of Ida 't Hooft), then two widths were put together; the lower one is sewn with ease against the upper one, and this gave one's arm more room. Flounces of lace decorated the sleeves.

The coiffure, brought into fashion by Madame de Fontange around 1680, became very popular (Plate 15). This headdress was often made completely out of lace and consisted of one or more flounces pleated and resting on the forehead. A cap encircled the back of the head and two lappets completed the whole. French needlepoint lace played a great part in this coiffure and this headdress had a long life as it remained fashionable from about 1680 till about 1720. During this same period, pelerines hanging to the middle of the back and 'tabliers' of lace were worn.

Prohibitions in England

'In England, where in 1649 the republic was proclaimed, the wearing of lace was forbidden; these regulations were respected by the lower classes and the middle class, but the puritanical higher classes continued to wear lace. Even Cromwell after his death (1658) was buried, dressed in the most beautiful purple, ermine and Flemish lace, even richer than most kings. In 1662 in the reign of Charles II the English parliament forbade the import of all lace, and the lace dealers were unable to provide the

22

court with enough 'English lace'. They tried to obviate this by bringing Flemish workers over to England to show English women how to make Brussels lace, but this undertaking did not succeed because the English linen thread was inferior and English women too inexperienced. At this time there was much smuggling from Brussels to England and in 1678 a ship was chartered by the Marquis of Nesmond, in which were brought over 744,953 yards of lace, with handkerchiefs, collars, fichus, aprons, dresses, gloves etc. all decorated with Point d'Angleterre (in reality Brussels lace).

'After this Brussels lace was seldom mentioned but became known as English lace, in order to make such smuggling possible' (Lefébure).

Eighteenth Century

In the eighteenth century ladies' dresses were lavishly made up with flounces of lace. The heavy Venetian and the Point de France competed with the lighter and suppler Alençon and Argentan lace. Of the bobbin laces the Brussels (so called Angleterre), the Mechlin, the Valenciennes, the Binche and the Chantilly became better known. An enormous amount of bobbin lace was used as the lighter aspect of these laces and their suppleness made pleating easier.

Tie ends, Barbes, Lappets

In ladies' costumes small coiffures came into fashion (Plates 19 and 20). These were made completely out of lace and the tie ends hanging below them were elegantly finished. These tie ends were often of different lengths an one could tell from that the rank of the wearer — the more important, the longer the tie ends. At the French court needlepoint lace was prescribed for grand gala. This belonged to the 'winterlace', while the so much lighter bobbin lace was proclaimed 'summerlace' (Plate 23). On the corsage several flounces of lace were worked, the decoration on the sleeves being especially noticeable, with perhaps as many as six flounces on each sleeve.

23

Pagodes, Engageantes, Pelerines, Tabliers

These flounces, named Engageantes and Pagodes, were narrow on the inside and with a width of five or six inches. Flounces in and around the décolleté, ruches round the neck, pelerines, tabliers, even whole dresses of lace were worn in the middle of the eighteenth century. An excellent example of this is the dress worn by Maria Theresa of Austria in the portrait painted by M. van Meijtens (Town Hall, Ghent). Children's clothing was also covered with lace at this time, with flounces on dresses, engageantes on sleeves, and it was usual for girls to wear a lace apron just like their mothers.

Quilles

In the second half of the eighteenth century the flounces were completely ruffled and sewn both down the length of a dress and across it. The laces which start narrowly on the shoulders ending in wide pieces at the bottom of the skirt are called quilles. They were fastened in pleats on both sides and were three or four yards long, about two inches wide at the top, to approximately six inches at the bottom.

Tournantes

The horizontal flounces, called tournantes, were just like the quilles and sewn on the dress on both sides in contrast with flounces, which were fastened on one side.

The Louis XVI coiffure had, next to feathers and ribbons also bows of lace; a voile often hung down at the back or in front of the cap or there would be a lace flounce hanging all the way round. In the eighteenth century the jabot stayed in fashion; to begin with still long and broad, but becoming smaller later on. In the middle of the eighteenth century a double lace flounce was worn, loosely gathered and falling on to the waistcoat from the shirt. According to Lefébure as much money was spent on lace in the eighteenth century as in the seventeenth century.

In 1738 the laces on the bed of the Queen of France cost

30,000 livres, and were made completely in Point d'Angleterre. The Duke de Luynes says in his memoirs that these bed-trimmings were renewed every year. In 1714, the dowager de la Ferté owned a footcover in Venise and a trimming for sheets in Argentan lace worth 40,000 écus, while the eldest daughter of Louis XIV received laces worth 625,000 francs, on the occasion of her marriage in 1739.

The French Revolution in 1789 brought a temporary stop to lace working; in France the lace industry was at a complete standstill and in a period of twelve years more than thirty large lace houses closed their doors. The muslins and other thin materials that had already been widely used in the time of Louis XVI, replaced completely the formerly fashionable laces in this revolutionary period and during the Directory. Shortly after the Directory (1795—1799) lace in France came into its own again, following Napoleon's wishes.

Nineteenth Century

At the wedding of Napoleon with Marie Louise of Austria the laces then used were valued by Felix Aubry in his report of 1851 as costing more than one million francs. Madame Récamier who gave a ball during the Consulate (1799—1804) where the first Consul made an appearance, did not receive her guests in the ballroom, since she was ill. Instead, each guest passed by her bedroom, which was according to the custom of those days next to one of the drawing-rooms. The loveliest woman of France rested on a gilded bed under curtains of beautiful Brussels lace; the footblanket matched the magnificent curtains and the embroidered batiste pillowcases were surrounded by flounces of Valenciennes lace. Madame Récamier herself wore a dress of the finest Brussels lace.

At Napoleon's coronation in 1804, he wore a jabot, a wavy collar and sleeve flounces, falling on to the hand, of Alençon needlepoint lace, in which the bee-motif was worked. He ordered a bed-trimming consisting of flounces, curtain and spread that was originally made for his wife Joséphine, but was finished for Marie Louise, and cost 40,000 francs (Lefébure). This was auctioned in May 1927 at Sotheby's in London; it was still in perfect condition.

As a consequence of the revival of the lace industry, lace was again used on clothing and in the home. Even so after 1815 lace disappeared from men's clothing and is only worn now on certain ceremonial occasions, Scottish evening-dress for instance.

Canezous, hat voiles, pelerines

In ladies' costume, however, lace again became important. The fashion-sheets edited in Paris and Brussels like 'Petit courrier des dames' and 'Le Conseiller des Graces' reproduced between 1820 and 1830 fashionable dresses decorated with huge collars, called pelerines, made of appliqué de Bruxelles, and canezous with long lappets of tulle brodé. Hats were made up with feathers and silk blonde lace and voiles, while wide lace scarves also were worn. There are still many beautiful specimens in the much richer Brussels bobbin lace, so called 'Drochel' to prove that this very expensive technique was still worked. Between 1830 and 1850 broad flounces appear on dresses, sewn on the skirts one, two or three above each other, and narrower ones on the corsage (Plate 21). Fashions under the Second Empire (1851–1870) gave every opportunity to display the beauty of the lace.

Volants, triangular shawls

Volants of appliqué on the skirt and a large triangular shawl in the same technique or a similar parure of Chantilly bobbin lace completed the costume of the social beauties of those days. Chemisettes, small collars and undersleeves were embroidered tastefully and trimmed with lace, and even stockings had pieces of lace inserted on the front of the leg; richly embroidered handkerchiefs were bordered with the broad Valenciennes lace. From 1870 to 1885 flounces became much more narrow, but they were used more generally on the afternoon and evening dresses.

Fichus

The fichu, a smaller triangular shawl, then coming into fashion, was made in the most superb quality of Mechlin or Valenciennes technique, while those of Brussels and Appliqué were well matched in beauty. Women enjoyed the gracious coquetry of the lace fan. The small lace cap that was still common up till the middle of the nineteenth century, was seen only occasionally after 1870; the lace coiffure, however flattering, had now disappeared completely, although some older ladies remained faithful to it. The late Queen-Mother of the Netherlands always wore a lace coiffure and her portraits will always remind us of this beautiful headdress, which gave an exceptional charm to the friendly face (Plate 14). In the last two decades of the nineteenth century, collars and cuffs reappeared on dresses in different forms; the large collar in cape or bertha form in particular was worn, made in the most beautiful needlepoint or bobbin lace. Around the hat and in front of the face veils were fashionable. There was already of course machine-made lace, but the real veils of Chantilly or Appliqué completed the afternoon dress which was trimmed with the same lace. The well-dressed woman used only hand-made lace in those days. The handkerchief, with a lace edging, had become smaller, but was still a traditional wedding gift.

Parasols

The parasol, made of Brussels needlepoint or bobbin lace, completed the outdoor costume, and also fashionable were the parasols of black Chantilly bobbin lace (Plate 34).

Twentieth Century, Dresses

In the early twentieth century fashions, lace predominates. Dresses that were still long until 1916 sometimes had lace overdresses or were made entirely of lace. An Austrian book on design 'Administration centrale Imp. et Roy. des Industries à domicile de Dentelles veritables, Vienne', edited in

27

1910, shows many designs of dresses, boleros, bags, collars etc. in needlepoint, bobbin and crocheted laces, made in Austria-Hungary; this found a ready sale in the suburbs of Paris and many seaside resorts. Between 1916 and 1930 lace was often worked luxuriously on short evening and afternoon dresses, with a lace corsage and silk skirt, or the other way round. A machine-made woven lace material was sometimes used, but the pretty dresses created by the big fashion houses were generally of hand-made lace. An expensive evening ensemble was completed with lace mittens, stockings with lace insertions and lace shoes and bags. The 1920's were a particularly good time for the lace trade and the lace workers of Europe, with visitors from North and South America who wanted to buy real lace from the old world. In 1935, the accent was again on collars, cuffs and jabots in the world of fashion, and it was easy to find the right lace for a particular style of dress; it was then a great luxury to have underwear trimmed with the fine Valenciennes and Point de Paris or even with Mechlin lace.

Cloths

Through American influence the use of cloths for lunch and afternoon tea increased. A lunch set, consisting of a centre-piece, napkins for everyone at table, lace mats and finger-bowl cloths has become an important item in many a household. Linen tablecloths and napkins often have beautiful lace borders. Sheets and pillowcases trimmed with lace as well as lace bedspreads even now are used, as in the seventeenth century.

Laces in Church

From early times lace has been used in churches. The precious needlepoint and bobbin laces that were worn by the Bishops are reproduced in paintings in their full splendour. The alb and surplice had a lace edging on the lower side of their sleeves (Plate 10). In the second half of the seventeenth century and in the eighteenth century flounce of the alb

was often more than a yard broad. An example of this expensive French needlepoint lace is in the possession of the Rijksmuseum. The Victoria & Albert Museum in London has in one of its show-cases an alb, decorated with Italian Point de rose. For services in Catholic churches, cloths (Plate 16), pallas, corporals, benediction cloths were, and still are used, and laces can also be seen on the antependiums and small altar frontals. In some Protestant churches there are laces along the cloths for the Lord's Supper, while in the Jewish synagogues at the circumcision rite cloths were used, sometimes adorned with laces. The lace collection of the Archbishops' Museum in Utrecht (housed in the Central Museum) shows the different kinds of laces used for ecclesiastical purposes. The Old Catholic Museum in Utrecht has in its show-cases albs and surplices with beautiful Flemish bobbin lace and Italian needlepoint laces, which give an impression of the luxury of the priest's clothing in the seventeenth and eighteenth century. Next to the lace ornaments already mentioned for church services there is also a Benediction cloth. Plate 44 shows a precious specimen of the end of the eighteenth century from the collection of the Boymans-Van Beuningen Museum.
Ornamental stitches in the ornament and in the clothing of the figures give a good impression of the contrast of light and shade in the drawing.

IV Needlepoint Laces

The Venetian Laces belong to the old needlepoint laces, starting with the Point Coupé.

VENETIAN NEEDLEPOINT LACES

Reticella

The straight bands and pointed edging had at first a completely geometrical composition and were called 'Reticella'. In the sixteenth century and the first half of the seventeenth century, all kinds of collars, cuffs, edgings for cloths etc. were made of this. The simple patterns consisted entirely of straight and round lines with a small triangle worked in buttonhole stitch for the close mesh part while the rest of the pattern consisted of festooned or cordoned lines (Plates 2 and 9).
The Rijksmuseum owns some collars and cloths of simple sizes and a beautiful Medicis or Stuart collar. This collar was made completely of linen, the fils tirés lines formed the squares and some threads of the linen, left in the squares when cut out, served as a base for the rest of the ornament. It seems as if the worker had been particularly enthusiastic with this collar for every square is filled in more beautifully than the next. The asymmetrical arrangement of the differently worked squares, placed in the quiet frame of the edging and points, gives it a special charm. Elisa Ricci calls this lace 'Punto a reticello' in her book 'Antiche trine Italiane'. To make this lace without a background of linen the worker pinned a pattern on to parchment or heavy dark coloured paper with the pinned holes close together. The pattern was laced tightly on to double linen and the worker sewed with needle and thread along the edge of the drawing, stitching down double thread, on which the lace was worked, in this way laying down 'the trace'. The rows of stitch forming the

close mesh parts of the ornament were fastened on to the double threads in the same way as the 'bars'.

In the second half of the sixteenth century and the first half of the seventeenth century laces were made using the geometrical patterns described above, while in the edging and in the points there would be either a symmetrical floral drawing or reproductions of human beings and animals. The square principal forms were sometimes alternately filled in with a comic figure, light of design, accentuated with a few threads but still full of expression in the outline. All these laces are called 'punto in area' by Elisa Ricci in her work 'Antiche trine Italiane' (to be translated by 'needlepoint lace'). In the illustrated work 'Die Sammlung Iklé several of these laces are reproduced.

Point de Venise plat

In the first half of the seventeenth century the pretty Venetian needlepoint lace came into being, now called 'Venise plat' to distinguish it from the kinds that followed. The drawing had a curling line as principal motif, from which flowers and leaves gracefully rose. These lines, flowers and leaves were mutually connected by festooned or sometimes cordoned bars running at random, decorated with picots, of which the fragment of a gentleman's jabot (Plate 12) is an excellent example. The small picots are thick closed projections, as contrasted with the picots of bobbin lace, made by a tiny open circle of twisted thread.

Ornamental stitches

In the 'Venise plat' the ornamental stitches give a richer

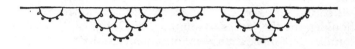

Lower edging of Venise plat, Venise à Relief and Venise à la Rose

31

Point de Venise plat

effect to the lace. The ornamental stitches were, just like the close mesh parts, worked in buttonhole stitch; but the stitches were grouped in such a way that they formed small patterns in which he open and closed mesh brought about a fine effect of light. The first Venetian seventeenth century needlepoint laces with the flower ornament were finished off on the outside by straight lines on which a severely stylised arched ornament formed the edge. This is to be seen as a reminder of the earlier geometrical drawings. In it was an endless variation of composition with or without picots, which will become clear when you have studied Plate 9, showing the collar and cuffs worn by Boudaen Courten.

Venise à relief - Venise à gros relief

Next to the 'Venise plat' two other laces came into being, becoming fashionable in the middle of the seventeenth century; namely the 'Venise à relief' and the 'Venise à gros relief'. This lace was particularly suitable for the men's costume, for with the beautiful 'Col rabat' (Plate 28) and the cravat (Plate 11), they were able to show off this lace in its full splendour. The circular collar was also worn round the shoulders in the ladies' costume. This collar and the sleeve flounces were more than mere ornaments to their clothes. The model on Plate 27 in bobbin lace shows that this collar gave an effective finish as in the heavy relief needlepoint lace

32

19. Coiffure, dress flounces and cuffs of Alençon needlepoint lace.

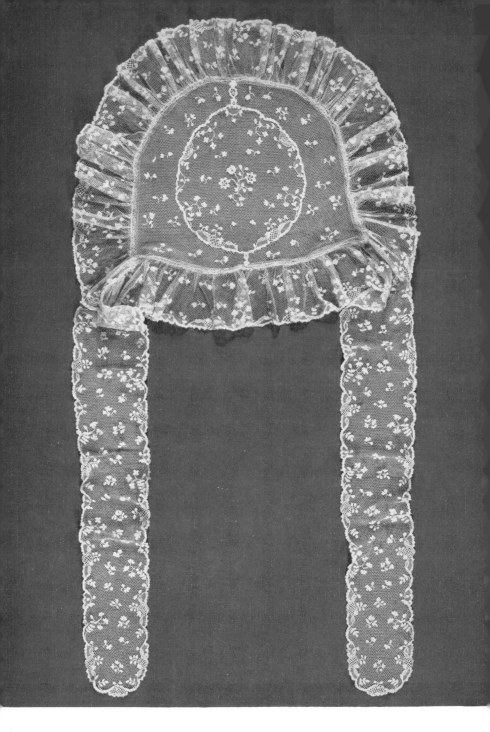

20. *Cap and lappets of Argentan needlepoint lace (second half 18th century).*

21. *Dress flounce, shawl and coiffure, most probably Appliqué de Bruxelles or Valenciennes bobbin lace (Marie Amelie, Queen of France, 1842).*

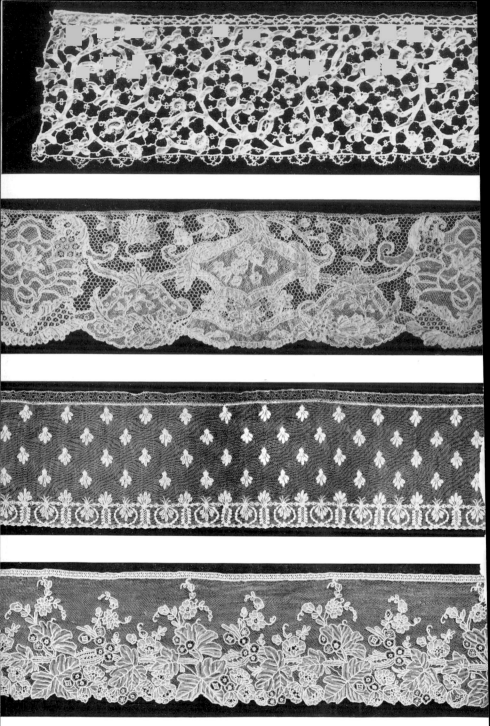

22. *Venise à la Rose needlepoint lace (c. 1700)*. 23. *Argentella needlepoint lace (c. 1740)*. 24. *Alençon needlepoint lace (c. 1810)*. 25. *Bruxelles needlepoint lace (c. 1820)*.

26. *Collar and dresspiece Flemish bobbin lace (c. 1640).*

27. Ladies' round collar Flemish bobbin lace (c. 1650).

28. *Col rabat Flemish bobbin lace. Sleeve flounces in gold lace (c. 1669).*

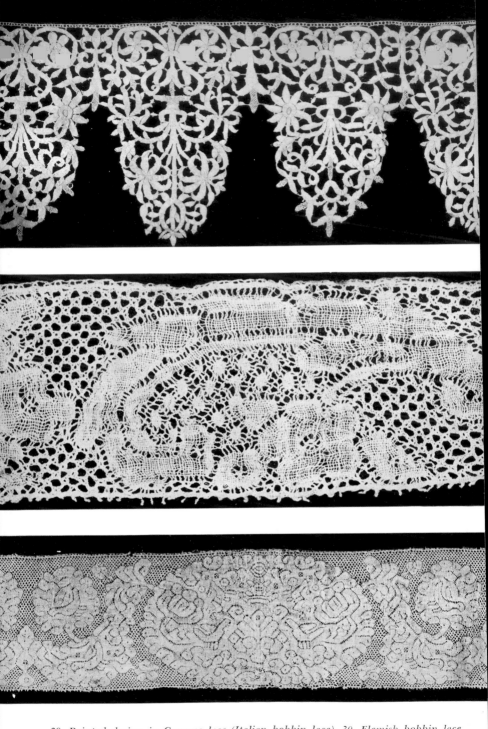

29. Pointed design in Genoese lace (Italian bobbin lace). 30. Flemish bobbin lace with square mesh (late 17th or early 18th century). 31. Dutch bobbin lace (second half 17th century).

(Plate 13). This Venise à relief had also played an important part in ladies' coiffures, as is shown so splendidly on Plate 15. Not only in society, but also in church clothing and for use in the service, the Venise à relief and à gros relief was a type of lace much in demand, for the heavier decorative ornament lends itself admirably to the church. The pointed lace on the alb of the priest (Plate 10) is the most typical lace of the second half of the seventeenth century and it is possible too that the flounce (Plate 13) was used in church services either on the clothing or on the communion bench or as a finish of the antependium.

With both laces, all the edges of the ornament had a more or less heavy relief, finished with picoted edgings. With the reliefs and ornamental motifs it seems as if there came into being light and shadow, giving a new effect to the lace, as if it had not grown from stitches but was cut from ivory. The flounce 'Venise à gros relief' (Plate 13) is an exquisite design, while the connecting bars have become real ornaments. This required great imagination from the designer and a skilled worker to make them. How far France has had influence on the Venise à relief lace after 1665 is uncertain. In spite of Italian distinguishing marks, we can not be sure how many of these beautiful collars and flounces were made

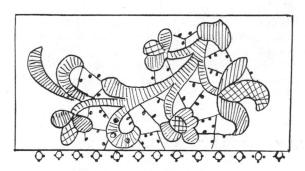

Pattern in point de Venise plat

in France, as after 1665 some thirty of the most able Venetian needlepoint laceworkers were employed, teaching French women in different workshops in France, owned by the government, the technical details of Venetian needlepoint lace.

Venise à la Rose or Point de Rose

In the lace we call Venise à la Rose the tendrils were fine and delicate and the flowers and leaves were small; the reliefs became less heavy, framed with round and oval figures, full of picots, giving to the lace a fine and ethereal look. The laceworker's art in Venice was at its most prosperous at the beginning of the eighteenth century with this kind of lace. The flounce (Plate 22), is an excellent example; the curling lines, the flowers with relief as well as the bars covered with small circles belong to the most beautiful ever made. The lower example too has repeats decorated with picots in abundance.

Venise au lacet

Of the Venise au lacet or Venetian lace with braid, that was made in the seventeenth century in Venice, beautiful specimens are to be found. These laces were used especially for church objects, as they are very effective from a distance. They did not take so long to complete as the 'Venise plat' or the 'Venise à relief'. The contours of the ornament were formed by a woven tape, that was either flat or round; it was sewn along the edges of the design and in this way used up the space that was otherwise filled in by a relief entailing a great amount of stitches similar to the rest of the Venetian laces.

FRENCH NEEDLEPOINT LACES

The lace industry became important in France and many

books and illustrated works are dedicated to French laces, particularly in the nineteenth century when lace again became the centre of interest. To the most important works belong: 'Histoire du Point d'Alençon' by Madame G. Despierres, 'Le poinct de France et les centres dentelliers au XVII et au XVIII siècle' by Madame Laurence de Laprade, as well as 'Broderie et Dentelles' by Ernest Lefébure.

According to Madame Despierres, needlepoint lace was called 'Velin' (parchment) in France because it was made on parchment. Needlepoint lace workers were called 'Vélineuses'.

Since its origin in the sixteenth century lace had been made in France, but it seems that in the seventeenth century the quality in Venice was much better, and so Venetian lace was much in demand at the French court. The prosperity of lace in France started during the reign of Louis XIV, who came to the throne in 1661. Ernest Lefébure writes in 'Broderie et Dentelles':

> 'The production and trade of all needlepoint lace was in Venice, and the French Court paid enormous sums for these, so the King with his Minister of Finance, M. Colbert, decided to import this wealthy industry to France. Colbert selected the cities where already lace was practised and proposed to establish workshops there with an exceptional privilege. The French Ambassador in Venice, Mgr. de Bonzy informed him: "Every monastery and all the poor families here find a living in the work" and in another letter "I see it is your plan to found the Venetian needlepoint industry in France; this could be done by sending daughters of the best workers here, to teach the French women" '.

Through Colbert a firm was founded in Paris in 1665, which for ten years had the sole right of fabrication, as well as an allowance of 36.000 livres. The first managers were Pluymers, Talon and another Talon, surnamed de Beaufort. The head-office and warehouse was established in Paris in the house of de Beaufort. The most important workshops came to be in Aurillac, Sedan, Reims, Le Quesnoy, Alençon, Argentan, Arras, Loudon, etc., and the thirty workers from Venice were divided amongst these workshops, while another two hundred laceworkers came from Flanders. Soon sixteen hundred French women were busy making lace in the newly acquired technique. In January 1673, Colbert wrote a letter to the Duke d'Aveaux, successor of Mgr. de Bonzy as French Ambassador in Venice, in which he says the following: 'I received the lace collar (le collet de point) worked in relief, that you sent me and I find it very beautiful. I compared it with the collars made in our workshops, but I must tell you at once, that our standard of lace making compares favourably with any other lace made in the Kingdom'. From this it is clear that in a period of eight years needlepoint lace in France had made great advances. To assist the national industry and to make the enterprise succeed, a regulation was laid down on the 12th October 1666, forbidding work on designs other than those of the workshops owned by the Government. The tradesmen were not allowed to transport Venetian, Genoese or other foreign laces, nor have them in stock, nor sell them in the kingdom, on penalty of confiscation of the goods and a fine of three thousand livres. From 20th January 1667, the King forbade all persons of standing to buy or wear foreign lace, on penalty of confiscation of the laces and a fine of fifteen hundred livres for disobedience. After 1675 de Beaufort's privilege came to an end, and new lace workshops were allowed to open with a choice of new patterns. In France there had come into being in those ten years a splendid industry, which could fully meet the demands of the lace trade.

Point de France

All the needlepoint and bobbin laces from whichever workshop they came, were called 'Point de France' in between the years 1665 and 1675 (Madame Despierres). But now only needlepoint laces made in France after 1665 are called 'Point de France', and these deviate from the design of Italian needlepoint lace of the same period. Technically Point de France was made in exactly the same way as the Venetian needlepoint lace and consisted of the buttonhole and the festoon stitch. The only difference was that the close mesh motifs were more often made in the festoon stitch than was the case with Venetian lace, which was made nearly without exception in the buttonhole stitch. That is why the solid parts of the French laces were closer and had a whiter and flatter effect. The great and wellknown designers, who planned the patterns for the Gobelin tapestries, and china, also created the designs for the lace workshops (Lefébure). These designs must have looked very much like the Italian patterns at first, for portraits painted after 1667 of French noblemen still show collars and jabots, differing very little from the Italian ones. According to Lefébure, when the artists Lebrun and Bérain worked on them, French needlepoint laces especially were given a very personal cachet. He continues by comparing very rightly the French needlepoint lace with the Italian laces made at the same time: 'In France the drawing is better balanced, more regular, powerful through an ideal architecture, while the symmetrical edgings wind to the left and to the right around a central, often symbolical motif'. The lower side of these laces were closed in to begin with by a straight edging of richly worked round of leaf figures while picoted bars formed the hexagonal background (meshes). Fine reliefs placed at random on the ornament heightened the beauty and accentuated the principal motifs. The restful symmetry of the French patterns is very striking. The lace on the cover of the book and on Plate 16 show very clearly the change in

Point de France

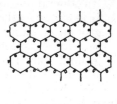

background
Point de France

37

the background; the hexagon can be clearly seen, although, because of the ornament, this is not always quite regular. Both these flounces can be seen in Amsterdam in the Rijksmuseum collection and are in excellent condition, although they are about 250 years old. The flounce on the cover of this book is a gift of the Society 'Het Kantsalet'.

In the collection of the Metropolitan Museum in New York is a particular jabot Point de France (Plate 17) which was worn in 1694 by the grandson of Louis XIV on the occasion of his marriage to Princess Marie Adelaide of Savoy. Over the whole surface of the jabot is portrayed a hunt of symmetrical composition, with the exception of the figures in the centre.

Old laces are still worn regularly and Plate 14 shows a portrait of H.M. the Queen-Mother of Holland, wearing at the beginning of the twentieth century French needlepoint lace made at the end of the seventeenth century or early in the eighteenth century.

Argentella, Argentan and Alençon

The elegant Point de France was predecessor to Argentella, Argentan and Alençon, where this needlepoint lace was made. Even in the eighteenth century one talked of Velin, meaning the Point de France, Alençon and Argentan lace, and it is difficult to say exactly what was made in one place and what in the other. Understandably, in places so close to each other it would be very similar and on studying the records, one realises how hard it is to distinguish them. Madame Despierres states in her very interesting book on page 100:

'In general one ascribes the lace, of which the background is made of meshes, to Alençon and the lace with a background of bars to Argentan. The first statement is right, but not the second, for the three kinds of bars as a background were made in both places, all stitches were and still are laid down in the same way, and they were made with the same materials'.

So it is impossible to state the difference between the barwork in Alençon and Argentan. The same workers worked for both places. Madame Despierres comes to the conclusion

38

that Point d'Argentan and Point d'Alençon were made in exactly the same way, but the workers in Alençon made all stitches and those in Argentan concentrated more on the bar background (Histoire du Point d'Alençon). Lefébure writes in the new edition of 'Broderie et Dentelles' on page 402:

'In the workshop in Argentan were also made all the designs that were worked in Alençon: Point Colbert, Point de France, simple or with diamond stitch, Point d'Argentan or d'Alençon. One specialised in the fabrication of the laces with an average background, less large than in the Point de France and larger than the ones made in Alençon. By the middle of the eighteenth century an Argentan worker had the idea of simplifying the work of the background by not festooning the preparatory basic stitch, on which the hexagonal mesh was formed, but by sewing round it. This mesh was called 'bride tortillée' in which the threads were twisted instead of the usual buttonhole stitch, and with it a huge amount of lace was immediately made. The lace workers from Alençon, who especially worked the small mesh in the eighteenth century, soon took over the new mesh from Argentan and that also was the origin of the particular demand in which the whole world could rejoice'.

From both quotations it is very clear that the two places made the same, that they helped each other with the execution, that Argentan specialised in the background of bars, and that it was a worker from Argentan who found out how to simplify the work of the bars, by sewing around the mesh instead of festooning it and that Alençon took over this mesh. In the light of this would it not seem best simply to call all laces with a festooned background 'Argentan-lace', and all laces with a background of small meshes also those with the sewn around mesh 'Alençon-lace'? The name of course merely indicates the type and not in this case necessarily where it is worked.

Argentella

From the Point de France the kind of lace named Argentella

has resulted; a needlepoint lace that gives on the whole a finer impression than the Point de France. The relief was brought back to just one thin festooned contour line, filled in with strong thread. The ornament had an exceptional wealth of ornamental stitches and left little room, or sometimes none at all, for the background; the close mesh motif was worked in festoon stitch, while the background became a hexagonal festooned mesh, mostly without picots. Although nothing impressive originates from this lace as from the Point de France, it still is a lace that demands our attention for its beauty. It has not been made since the middle of the eighteenth century. Plate 35 shows an excellent example of this.

Argentan

Closely related to the Argentella was the Argentanlace, worked in the same way, but deviating from it through the smaller proportion of the festooned mesh; it was always without picots. Up to the second half of the eighteenth century the ornamental stitches were still worked in the lace in a rich variety, but in the Louis XVI period, when the ornament becomes more refined and the background takes up more room, the variety is less (Plate 20). The ornamental stitches each had their own name in the eighteenth century as is shown on Plate IV in the book of Madame Despierres and they still live among the lace workers under those names. Lace had become plainer in the last quarter of the eighteenth century as is made clear by the cap in Plate 20, but to be able to value the refinement and labour of the background, the relief and the close mesh motifs to the full, one only has to look at the small flowers and the oval figures in the edging. Lefébure writes:

'Even in the Empire period, Argentanlace is made again under the personal patronage of the Emperor Napoleon I, who tried to breathe new life into the lace industry. Later, after a short period of decline, he tried to found the lace industry anew in the former lace centres, led by the house Lefébure, as a source of income for the people and as a

40

special French art expression. Napoleon III also took much interest in this aspiration'.

Alençon

The Alençonlace has known a prosperity that was as great or greater than the Argentan. As they were both made at the same time, the ornament was the same, but the Alençon had a finer background. This background consists of a rectangular mesh with rows of stitches of the upper side running to the lower side of the lace. These were made by rows of buttonhole stitches and after each of these, the meshes were sewn around once to go back to the beginning. The ornamental stitches and the close mesh motifs were worked in the same way as those of the Argentanlace.

When the Alençonlace contained an ornament of tendrils at the end of the Louis XV period, decorated with small oval leaves, horsehair was mostly used to fill in the relief, through which it stood out stiffly and so gave a richer and accentuated edge to the flowers and leaves. These Alençonlaces were worked on costumes used for gala occasions in the eighteenth century, for both men and women, while children too wore these expensive laces.

In a painting (Plate 18) called 'The Astronomer' by Lepice, we can see the beautiful Alençon flounces hanging from the waistcoat and out of the sleeves. These must have been made about 1760. The portrait of Margaretha Trip by J. M. Quinkhard (1688—1772) (Plate 19), reproduces the same lace on cap and dress and shows the elegance of making up and

Edging Alençon, 18th Century

wearing a cap and fichu. Plate 24 is Alençon in an Empire pattern with a much more sober design, a bee design, although ornamental stitches in small stylised motifs are worked.

ITALIAN NEEDLEPOINT LACE

Burano

Venice, that had in the eighteenth century resisted the competition of the Argentan- and Alençonlace, also made a lace with a background which was very strongly influenced by both these French needlepoint laces, in particular by the Alençonlace. On viewing the Plates of the excellent work by Elisa Ricci in 'Antiche Trine Italiane', but even more on studying the Burano laces, one can see at once the difference from the above-mentioned French laces. The close mesh motifs of the ornament were often made in typical Italian buttonhole stitch, while the pretty ornamental stitches were mostly too large in proportion. Flowers, consisting partly or entirely of bordered 'spiders' (a term given to a special motif), formed a light contrast to the background and also varied from the Alençon because of the much more irregular working.

BELGIAN NEEDLEPOINT LACES

In the beginning of the eighteenth century the Southern Netherlands made exceptionally artistic lace, of which the ornament was needlework and the background was bobbined while the Brussels needlepoint lace was famous in the nineteenth century.

It is difficult to believe that needlepoint lace had never been made before in Flanders, but we have little evidence to confirm this. An article devoted to needlepoint laces made in the Netherlands in the seventeenth and eighteenth century appeared in the Bulletin of the Musées Royaux d'Art et d'Histoire in Brussels, written by Madame Paulis, at that time Assistant Librarian at the Museum. She writes:

'Several Italian pattern books, especially the work by Cesare Vecellio, called "Corona delle nobile et virtuose done" that appeared in Venice in 1617 and "l'Ornamente nobile" by Lucretia Romana, edited in the same city in 1620, give some drawings under the name of "Ponti fiaminghi" or "Ponti in aria fiaminghi". So in the beginning of the seventeenth century Flemish needlepoint lace did exist and its fame reached as far as over the borders.'

She continues a little further on:

'As the patterns of the Flemish bobbin lace do not differ much from the Italian ones, the technical execution most probably was not similar. We think that the Flemish then already had quality and fine workmanship and this was maintained. The Italian lace had a very close weave and the Flemish a very light one.'

After explaining the Italian weaves in detail, she comes to the conclusion that the above mentioned museum in Brussels most probably also owns the lighter worked Flemish needlepoint laces among the early seventeenth century ones. She finds it impossible to believe that the needlepoint lace industry would have ceased in the seventeenth century, to appear again at the beginning of the eighteenth century with such splendid laces, and she hopes to solve the problem by labelling the laces, with a design like the Venise plat or the Venise à la Rose, but of a looser technique, as Flemish needlepoint laces.

Flemish needlepoint lace, seventeenth century

In contrast to the Italian laces, Flemish lace has an easily recognisable loose working and also an openworked edging.

Brussels needlepoint lace, eighteenth century

Madame Paulis continues her article on eighteenth century

needlepoint laces, by supposing, after quoting various sources, that in the eighteenth century Brussels must have had an important needlepoint lace industry, in spite of the fact that so little of it is left. As has been said before, several splendid examples of a mixed kind of lace are left in many a collection, of which Plate 46 shows a royal lappet from the middle of the eighteenth century. The ethereal fine needlepoint lace, of which the ornament is made, is held by what is known as a 'Drochel' background, made with the bobbins in-between the motifs.

Brussels needlepoint lace, nineteenth century

Better known is the Point de Gaze or Point de Bruxelles from the nineteenth century, which was made in large quantities especially after 1830. To begin with it was made with linen thread but after the import of cotton thread to the lace industry, it was made mostly in the cheaper cotton material. Collars, shawls, broad and narrow flounces, handkerchiefs, fans and parasols, even whole dresses in every kind of design were made from it, for home use as well as for export. Brussels needlepoint lace is softer than the Alençonlace, because the background is thinner. This was and still is laid out by rows of buttonhole stitches going back and forth, through which the mesh partly consists of only one thread. The close mesh motif is worked in festoon stitch around a strained thread, while the thin relief is fastened lightly along the edges with the same stitch. Plate 25 shows a flounce of the first part of

Brussels needlepoint

English needlepoint

the nineteenth century, while Plate 21 portrays Queen Marie Amélie, wife of Louis Philippe, King of France from 1830 to 1848, dressed in fine Brussels lace.

In the second half of the nineteenth century the drawing often shows a relief flower, consisting of two or three leaves worked together, that are sewn on to the flower. This special mark has been preserved up to the present day.

ENGLISH AND IRISH NEEDLEPOINT LACE

England owes the revival of its lace-work to the Flemish and French refugees, who came to England to seek religious freedom. They settled mainly in Cranfield, Olney, Buckingham, Newport Pagnell and Stony Stratford.

A pattern book by Vinciolo appeared in 1599 in English and in 1632 a pattern book called 'Shorleykers Scholehouse for the needle' — a picture book of English lace (edition in the Victoria & Albert Museum, London).

In the sixteenth and seventeenth centuries characteristic needlepoint laces were made in England with an ornament totally different from that on the continent; although according to Mrs. Bury Palisser (Page 321) most laces worn in the second half of the sixteenth century in England were of Flemish origin. Prohibitions to import lace were issued under the reigns of Henry VIII and of his daughter Elizabeth, who tried in this way to support the industry of the country. The first prohibitions date from 1546, but notwithstanding this, the annual import of trimmings, bobbin lace, etc. still amounted to £10,000 in 1546, according to Pierre Verhaegen (Les industries à domicile en Belgiques, Page 40). A beautiful collection of English laces can be seen in the Victoria & Albert Museum, London. Three interesting proof cloths are dated 1654, 1666, 1696, of which the one of 1666 has workings in the Reticella technique. The seventeenth century needlepoint lace flounces, in which the English rose and the thistle are worked as an ornament, have a heavier composition and are less fine than those of the continent, although the method is identical. There are also a few small panels with a biblical representation, among others of Adam and Eve in Paradise, of which the edging is typically English, with English flowers as well as the unicorn and the lion pictured on it. Another, 'Solomon's Judgement' is distinguished through its relief and its finish with small pearls from laces that were made in Italy and France.

Irish crochet, which became a national industry in the second half of the nineteenth century, was started about 1845 by the Sisters of the Ursuline Convent in County Cork as a suitable work for the poor children in their schools. By the 1870's there were more than 12,000 women occupied with crochet lace in the neighbourhood of Cork. They copied the heavy Venetian Rose point laces and produced some striking effects with this technique.

GERMAN NEEDLEPOINT LACE

The finer German needlepoint lace first dates from 1855 when the German Government helped to import Brussels needlepoint lace in the Kreis Hirschberg as a home industry, by advancing to a wholesale lace dealer in Berlin about 30,000 marks free of interest and for eight years giving him an annual subsidy of about 1650 marks. That was the foundation of lace work in Germany and it kept 1400 women employed in 1859, but after that under different managements the lace industry had many ups and downs. Maria Theresa von Ples, who took over the whole institution in 1911 from Frau Dobeneck and Frau Bardt, dedicated herself completely to lace work in Hirschberg. Frau Dobeneck and Frau Bardt had different workshops in the years 1906–1911, during which time they added their own artistic ideas to the lace. Technically, the finish of the lace resembles the Brussels needlepoint lace of the nineteenth century. (The above information was obtained from a brochure, edited with reference to an exhibition in Haarlem in May 1912 in the Museum for Applied Arts.)

V Bobbin Laces

Bobbin lace came into being in the beginning of the sixteenth century, according to the many pattern books giving several designs for this technique. It is not known where bobbin lace first started as we have no historical facts. We know Italy was making it at that time and also Flanders, while Germany and France were not far behind. In Flanders bobbin lace developed very rapidly, and the technique was speeded up to an extraordinary extent. Bobbin lace consists of three basic stitches namely, the linen stitch, the net stitches and the Point d'esprit also called Point de reprise or leaves type. On reading this it sounds very simple to learn but the endless variations of these stitches and the difficulties that correct execution of the design entails, are far more complicated than the simple statement of three basic stitches leads one to suppose. Because of this, the laceworker generally prefers to practise only one kind of lace, and although it may of course happen that she has to deviate from that, this is rare. With only one technique to practise, the worker can become very skilled, and able to produce the most beautiful lacework in the shortest possible time, so the manufacturer for whom she works will pay very high wages for this work.

Bobbin lace can be divided into two principal groups, with an enormous difference in technique, as follows:

A. By which the worker fastens the required number of bobbins above the parchment already pricked with the design, and firmly pinned to a lacemakers cushion. While plaiting and twisting the threads, and putting in the pins to hold the lace in position as the worker progresses with the design, the threads interweave to form both the motifs and the background of the lace.

B. Laces for which the pattern is drawn in lines on the special lacemakers cardboard. Each motif is made separately with

47

the bobbins while the worker chooses the spacing of the pins herself; for the joining together of the motifs to form the lace, 'sewings' with a pin or very fine hook are made. The background and the ornamental motifs are worked with separate bobbins in-between the ornament, and are fastened with this hook where necessary. ('Sewings' are again used to join the lace motifs and the background.)

THE LACES BELONGING TO GROUP A

Italian bobbin laces

The laces in a bar pattern of the sixteenth and seventeenth centuries are very thin and lend themselves admirably to the finish of 'millstone-collars', cuffs and ladies' caps. The lace round the filet cloth (Plate 3) is an excellent example of these early bobbin laces, having a geometrical foundation and the bobbins at the same time forming the edge. On the collars (Plates 4 and 7) is shown the same pattern while a different composition in this bobbin lace is fastened to apron and dress on the children's portrait (Plate 6).

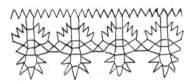

Pattern in Italian bobbin lace

The laces with few motifs or completely in Point d'esprit are more massive and closely resemble needlepoint lace; but on studying these one can see that the ornament does not consist of rows of stitches, but that it is one thread, running

48

32. *Valenciennes bobbin lace (mid 18th century). 33. Binche bobbin lace (mid 18th century).*

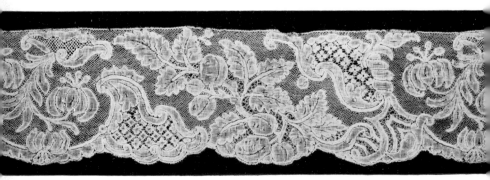

34. *Parasol of Chantilly silk bobbin lace (c. 1875). 35. Mechlin bobbin lace (mid 18th century).*

36. *Dutch national costume cap. Lille bobbin lace (19th century).*

37. Lace coiffure worn in a hat. (Queen Anna Pavlovna as Princess of Orange).
38. Fan in Chantilly bobbin lace (second half 19th century).

39. *Coiffure and dress attire of black Blonde bobbin lace (Queen Maria Louisa of Spain).*

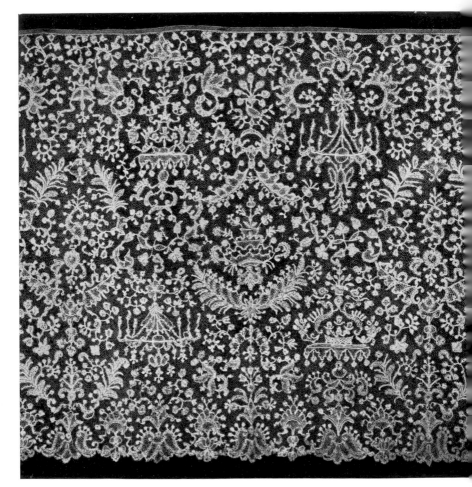

40. *Flemish bobbin lace, made in parts — group B (17th century). 41. Broad flounce Brussels bobbin lace (early 18th century).*

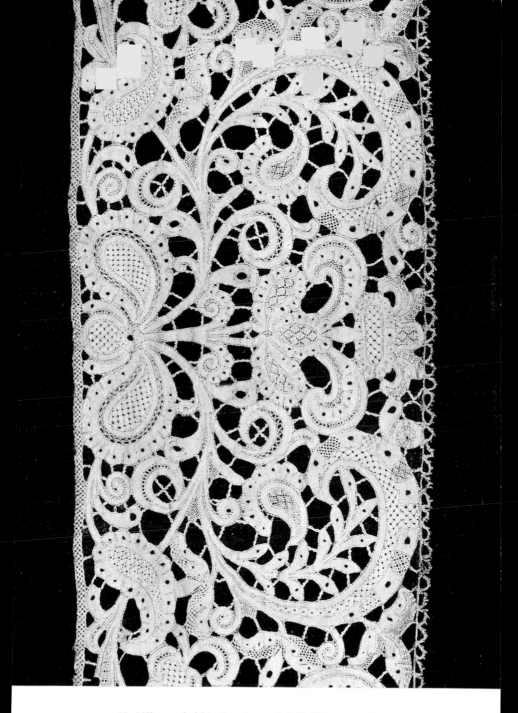

42. *Milanese bobbin lace (second half 17th century).*

43. Broad Alb flounce Brabants bobbin lace (early 18th century).

Pattern in Italian bobbin lace

over and under a number of other threads and in this way
giving a ribbed effect. They are heavy and were also worked
on the seventeenth century flat collars. Plate 29 shows a
reproduction of an exceptionally pretty Genoese lace, entirely
made in Point d'esprit. Genoa, very well known in the seventeenth century for its lace industry, also followed those
patterns with the exception of the above-mentioned lace.
N. Hudson Moore writes in 'The Lace Book' on Page 82, that
'in many royal inventories Genoese lace was mentioned, and
Maria de Medicis owned a great deal. These laces were of silk
or linen, for the Genoese republic had issued laws regulating
the wearing of gold and silver lace'.

Gold and Silver Laces

About the gold and silver laces of the sixteenth century he
continues: 'They were made all over Italy in Milan, Florence,
Genoa, Lucca and Venice'. Pierre Verhaegen says in his work
'Les industries à domiciles' on Page 31 'that both Spain and
France concentrated on the fabrication of gold and silver
lace'. To appreciate the importance men as well as women
attached to gold laces for decoration, one only has to look at
one of the group of the Banquet of the Civil Guard, painted
by Van der Helst in June 1648 (Rijksmuseum).
Several yards of gold lace are inserted on jacket and trousers,
showing above the top of the boots. That there is so little

49

left is not only because of the extravagance of such laces, but because they disappeared in the melting-pot, as it was real gold and silver thread of which those guipures were made. On the portrait of the boy (Plate 28) flounces of this gold lace are put on the sleeves, resting on the white under-sleeves. Gold and silver lace is also often used for the clothing of priests and for the altar.

Flandreslace, Fond à cinq trous

The laces made in Flanders were called 'Flandreslace' in the seventeenth century. To the most beautiful of these belong the Louis XIV patterns with the heavy oval principal motif and the branches running symmetrically to both sides. The background of this lace consists of square meshes, running one into the other diagonally, and known as *Fond à cinq trous* or square mesh.

'Flandreslace' is sometimes called Trolle lace; according to Pierre Verhaegen the name derives from the West-Flemish word 'drol' meaning 'coarse thread', but some years ago one of the greatest lace manufacturers thought that the word 'Trolle' came from the Brussels-Flemish word 'trolies', meaning bars with which the laceworkers indicate the background. The Flandreslace with fond à cinq trous was made in the eighteenth and nineteenth centuries, and is still exported from Flanders to-day. It is made with or without a thick gimp thread around the ornament (Plate 30). On the portrait of the son of Admiral van Nes (Plate 28), the boy wears a col rabat trimmed with beautiful Flemish bobbin lace, and the ladies' collar (Plate 27) is also an outstanding example of this lace, so often used in the Netherlands in the middle of the seventeenth century. An unusual factor with all these collars is that the lace was sewn out of a straight flounce which is why pleats were made in the corners.

Dutch Lace

Closely related to Flemish lace is the so-called 'Dutch lace' showing the same ornament, but with a different stitch for

50

the background. The diagonal and lengthwise lines, each of two threads, are plaited around each other in such a way that every hole is closed in by a hexagonal weave (Plate 31). Both these laces, the Flemish and the Dutch, are rather massive in their forms, very flat and close of technique and the fine open outlines joining the motifs, which give the flowers such a clear design, show the difficulties that the lace-worker has to face in order to make such an impressive pattern with so little contrast.

'Dutch lace' was often used in Holland in the seventeenth century, which is why it was given this name, and in the eighteenth century the Point de Paris was developed from it; the background has the same form although it is more open.

Flemish Lace

There was still only one lace worked in Flanders in the seventeenth century, with no background, but consisting solely of flowers that were separated by twisted 'bars' and which was certainly a predecessor of the Valenciennes lace, so much in demand during the Rococo- and Louis XVI periods, although attributed to the Flandres group. This lace was used for clothing in straight bands and with scalloped edges.

Valenciennes Lace

That the first Valenciennes lace resembles the seventeenth century Flandres is very understandable, for according to M. A. Malotet *(La dentelle à Valenciennes)* 'a certain Françoise Badard went from Valenciennes to Antwerp from 1639 till 1644 to learn lace work there and once back in Valenciennes she settled there and became a promoter of the lace industry'. Pierre Verhaegen *(Les industries à domicile)* writes:

'the women who came to France from Flanders under the reign of Louis XIV have had a great influence on Valenciennes lace, which, according to Mrs. Bury Palisser, was already made there in the fifteenth century. It was certainly the Flemish influence that gave the lace the definite character of a close worked ornament, which has

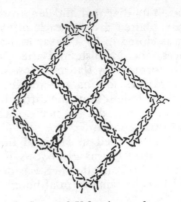

Background Valenciennes lace

been maintained. The French Revolution destroyed the industry in Valenciennes, which moved to Belgium, where it was already known. In 1896, in the town of Bruges, two thousand workers were still kept busy with the bobbin made Valenciennes lace'.

A speciality of the Valenciennes background mesh was that it could be worked with either a square or round holed mesh. In the eighteenth and nineteenth centuries chiefly the former, the square mesh was mostly worked. For all lines formed by these meshes, four threads are needed, plaited together several times, and for this reason many bobbins are needed. The ornament is completely in linen type and the prettier quality is bobbined so close that it is difficult to distinguish the threads which sometimes gives it an impression of paper. Plate 32 shows a flounce made in the eighteenth century with a very fine thread; the lace worker must have great knowledge and skill to make such flounces, which are about three inches wide and need approximately 600 bobbins. Nowadays, the narrower laces are very fashionable in France for underwear, because these fine but still extremely hardwearing laces make an attractive adornment for an article that has to be perpetually washed and ironed.

52

Binche Lace

The Binche lace originated from the same source as the Valenciennes and is, according to Pierre Verhaegen very similar to begin with; Savary says 'that these laces and the Flemish ones are alike'. The Binche was already known in the late Louis XIV period by its underground of spiders, often different in size and form, giving the lace a gay appearance. The ornament was worked in linen stitch, not so close as that of the Valenciennes lace; this brought about a subtle distinction between the two laces. The net type was introduced in the rich ornament of those days in the Regency period. The interchange of linen and net type gave much more colour variation, and this so characteristic division of light and shade next to the spider-background has been preserved in the Binche up to the present day. This was the lace of the Regency and Rococo period, together with the Brussels lace (Plate 33).

Pierre Verhaegen, who has in his work assembled so many facts of all the Belgian laces, writes: 'Binche left the older industry in the middle of the nineteenth century to concentrate on a simpler kind of lace'. When his book was published there were only nine older workers left, who were kept busy with bobbin lace.

The fabrication of the Binche lace has been moved to the province of Antwerp; with good new designs, based on beautiful old patterns, fine Binche laces are still made under the new name of 'Point de Fée'.

Mechlin Lace

In the beginning of the eighteenth century the town of Mechlin gave its name to a very expensive lace which was, according to Pierre Verhaegen, much in demand at the French court under Louis XV and in the first half of the eighteenth century in England. Mrs. Lowes states in her work: 'Chats on Old Lace': 'In 1699 in England, it was already a much valued lace; Queen Mary used considerable quantities and Queen Anne once bought 83 yards for £247.' The prominent distinguishing mark of the lace of the eighteenth century and of the later Mechlin lace is the thick thread, called a gimp thread, surrounding the whole ornament as a contour; every flower and leaf is worked in cloth stitch, but this has been accomplished with such a striking irregularity, that it gives the lace an unexpected sparkle. The background is hexagonal fine mesh, of which two lengthwise sides are plaited out of four threads, while the other sides consist of two threads twisted around each other.

In the Louis XV period the ornamental stitches were raised to a nearly endless variation, making the richness of the design clearer (Plate 23).

In the same period Mechlin laces were also made, deviating from the prototype of the eighteenth century, as far as the background was concerned. For there are laces with a spidery ground, that were completely bobbin-made in the net mesh; and also others with a hexagonal mesh as background, and an extra thick gimp thread around the ornament. It seems that these kinds were made in order to compete with the Binche and with the French Alençonlace. The late Louis XV laces have less ornament and much more background, with proportionally small ornamental stitches.

The Louis XVI flounces, with the ornament of small flowers, leaves and bud-spots, lent themselves particularly to the pleated ornamentation of the light summer materials that were often worn at that time. Flounces with Empire and Louis Philippe ornament, as well as fichus from the Second

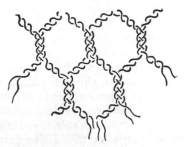

Background Mechlin lace

54

Empire (1851—1871) are preserved. Because of the number of bobbins that this lace requires, Mechlin lace is rarely wider than six inches.

The town of Mechlin had only a few old workers left in the middle of the nineteenth century; while a school, opened in 1906, under the supervision of Mademoiselle De Costenoble, who was an able laceworker, had to close its door some years later, as girls could earn more in other industries.

According to Pierre Verhaegen, the not very flourishing industry was then moved to Turnhout. The great illustrated work by E. van Overloop, '*Matériaux pour servir à l'histoire de la dentelle en Belgique*' contains reproductions of many of the eighteenth century Mechlin laces from the collection of the Musées Royaus des Arts Décoratifs et Industriels in Brussels.

Chantilly Lace

Chantilly lace originated in France near Paris, becoming very well-known when worked in black silken thread. Madame de Maintenon (1635—1719) wears a coiffure of fine black lace in the painting by Ferdinand Elle (Musée de Versailles). In the eighteenth century, fichus of black lace were pleated over white lace bonnets and fastened under the chin. In the painting by Quinkhard (Rijksmuseum, Plate 19) this double luxury coiffure is worn. A pastel by Liotard in the Rijksmuseum of Mrs. Boere portrays the beauty of a cape and dress in black Chantilly lace. The large proportions of the cape with the exceptionally rich design on the fine background show the great achievements in the art of lace by 1746.

In the nineteenth century, in the period of Empress Eugénie (1852—1870), women wore black lace flounces on dresses and a triangular black Chantilly shawl was considered necessary to complete a beautiful toilet.

Collars, fans (Plate 38), parasols (Plate 34), mittens etc. were made in the most luxurious designs.

The lace industry, that was on the decline near Paris because of the French Revolution, was, according to Lefébure, taken to Caen and Bayeux in Normandy around 1835, where it attained a refinement never reached before. In South and East Belgium too a flourishing Chantilly-industry developed. Pierre Verhaegen writes that there were 49 lace schools in Grammont in 1851, where this kind was taught so that one even talked of Grammont lace. There was also a good export trade to Spain and South America of the Chantilly laces. This lace distinguished itself from other laces because the background was bobbin-made in hexagonal mesh, consisting of two threads twisted around each other, while the motifs were completely worked in the net type and surrounded by a thick gimp thread. It was the invention of an invisible connection, according to Pierre Verhaegen (*Les industries à domicile*) which made it possible to work individual motifs separately — thus simplifying the working — later to be joined by the invisible stitch called 'Point de raccord'.

Blonde Lace

The Blonde lace, that like the Chantilly was worked in silk thread, owes its name to the colour of the Nanking silk. In the eighteenth century it was the 'fine Blonde', which as Lefébure says was 'so willingly worn by Marie Antoinette'; but the 'Spanish Blonde' with great sparkling satin-like flowers, was a lace especially of the nineteenth century. Plate 19 shows Marie Louise, Queen of Spain in a dress and coiffure with beautiful black silk lace after a painting by Goya. That satin-like glow of the ornament in the lace was obtained by the turning threads of the cloth stitch being much thicker than those of the flower. The mesh of the background corresponds with the Chantilly. It was a brilliant lace, but easily torn as the background was exceptionally fine. The fashion magazines of 1820—1830 recommended all kinds of trimmings of this excellent Blonde lace as particularly elegant and modern.
According to M. Hudson Moore in *The Lace Book,* the white and black silk Blonde laces worn by Empress Eugénie in the painting by Winterhalter were sold in 1903 in London for 45 guineas. In the work of Carlier de Lantsheere *Trésor de l'art dentellier,* Blonde laces are also mentioned under the name of 'dentelle de Grammont, de Caen et de Bayeux'.

Point de Paris

The Point de Paris originated in the eighteenth century near Paris and runs completely parallel with the Chantilly; in his work *Broderie et Dentelles* Lefébure does in fact give an example of a lace with a fond 'Point de Paris' as if it was Chantilly lace. But in the nineteenth century, when the industry had moved to Belgium, the lace with this particular background took the name of Point de Paris. The background of this lace consists of hexagonal holes, surrounded by the triangles; it is worked with two threads twisted round each other between the crossings. Except for the hexagonal and triangular form in the background, the lace has a thick gleaming gimp thread around the motif which distinguishes it from the background. Even now in the twentieth century the flowerbasket is still the principal motif, although it has been adapted to later fashions and has also been improved by beautiful bird designs. For clerical use symbolical motifs and cherubs are a popular part of the design. The illustrated work *Trésor de l'art dentellier* by Carlier de Lantsheere, reproduces a great amount of Point de Paris laces, with the names by which they are known, like 'Les Anges', 'Le Chandelier', 'Le vaste antique' etc.

Lille Lace

The Lille laces are secondary in quality to the Point de Paris, but the design has a rich aspect.

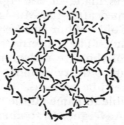

Mesh Point de Paris

57

This lace originated in the North of France in the eighteenth century and in the nineteenth century was a thriving industry not only in France but in Belgium too. Lille lace was also made in England (Buckingham) and in Denmark (Schleswig-Holstein) where this industry was transferred in the nineteenth century. The background is the same round mesh characteristic of Chantilly and the Blonde, the ornament which is surrounded by a thick gimp thread is nearly always in the linen or cloth stitch. It was bobbin-made in linen thread and in the nineteenth century in cotton thread too. Many ornamental stitches add to the beauty of the flower design, especially of the English ones, while the Belgian and the French Lille patterns have more generally an ornament of small flowers and leaves.

Apart from being used for ladies' costumes, and in the nineteenth century as beautiful narrow flounces for baby bonnets, these Lille laces were much in demand in the eighteenth and nineteenth centuries in the Netherlands, for the caps of the national costumes. So arose a great and lively export of these laces to that country, and it was known not only as Lille lace in the trade, but also as Dutch lace. The ornament for these caps has hardly changed at all in the nineteenth century. Branches with flowers or baskets with flowers form the principal motif for these laces. Plate 36 shows a lace cap from a Dutch national costume.

Cluny Laces

In the second half of the nineteenth century the name Cluny was given to the laces made in Auvergne out of a coarser thread. This was named after the Musée de Cluny in Paris, where some pieces of old bobbin lace were kept (E. Lefébure, *Broderie et Dentelles*). The patterns are inspired by the geometrical designs of the lace collars and cuffs of the sixteenth and seventeenth century. A more specific design later on has now led to the cube patterns.

It would not be possible to name all the villages where Cluny laces were made — Auvergne, Craponne, Mirecourt and in The Vosges in France and also in Belgium, North-Italy,

Switzerland, Austria, Germany, Holland, Russia, Sweden, Denmark. These laces were also transferred to Malta and Ceylon, Shanghai, Japan and Indonesia (Sumatra). They all look alike but an experienced eye can tell the difference by the thread and the 'local' technique.

THE LACES BELONGING TO GROUP B

The laces belonging to this group are worked in parts, namely first the motif, and then the background. The design has to be worked out beforehand in such a way that the whole can be divided in pieces to be joined later. The designer has to consider not only a striking and elegant design, but also one technically possible to convert into this type of lace. This type of lace is also made in Honiton.

Milanese Lace

Milanese lace dates from the seventeenth century. Lace was made in Milan before this, and Marie Schuette says in her work 'Alte Spitzen', quoting Elisa Ricci. 'that the numerous Milanese acts issued at the end of the sixteenth and seventeenth century against luxurious clothing, expressly prohibit needlepoint and foreign laces, leaving free on the contrary, the gold and silver laces of the local industry'. The characteristic ornament of these seventeenth-century laces worked with thread (Plate 41) is built out of a continuous curling band of an identical or nearly identical width, enclosed on both sides by a small open-worked edging. The very close cloth or linen weave of the band is interrupted only occasionally by a few holes, while ornamental stitches appear only once in a while. The background consists of either bars or meshes while the oldest ones have no background. When it was of meshes then they were either round or square: the round mesh in-between the motif, made with as many bobbins as were needed to fill in the space; the square one only demanded one pair of bobbins, connected by the worker plaiting zigzag, with the

59

indispensable hook. The prettiest baroque patterns are worked up with ornamental stitches in the Milanese technique especially for clerical use (Plate 41).

Milanese lace with string

In the seventeenth century Milanese bobbin lace was imitated. These are the laces that were called 'Milan au lacet' or 'Milanese with the string' or 'guipure'. The bobbin-made motif was replaced by the woven lacet, while the background and the fillings were put in-between by needle: this imitation shows wrinkles in the corner through the pleating of the band; a good kind of lace, but in quality it is not to be compared with the Milanese lace bobbin-made by hand. (According to French custom the name 'guipure' is for lace with the ground of meshes; by contrast E. van Overloop means lace without a background.)

Flandreslace

As mentioned earlier, all laces made in Flanders were called Flandreslace in the seventeenth century. To prevent confusion for the layman, Flemish lace made in one piece was later called 'Flandres with fond à cinq trous'. (I believe that it was Mr. E. van Overloop, Curator and Chef des Musées Royaux d'Art et d'Histoire, who first used this name.)
This Flemish lace was used around 1600 in narrow bands on the ladies' hats; around 1615 beautiful frilled lace appeared on the collars and cuffs, and gentlemen wore these flounces out of ridingboots, the so called canons. Paintings by Van Dyck, Santvoort, Hals and their contemporaries show the beautiful Flemish bobbin laces that were worn in the Netherlands. The portrait of Charles I painted by Van Dyck is a rare example of the quality of lace; it shows the King in three attitudes, namely full face and both profiles, wearing a different collar for each pose. With these Louis XIII collars from the first part of the seventeenth century every point was a closed, severely stylised, floral ornament, of which the motifs were made separately and set together with a hook by small

60

connections, while working. In 1625 the designs were still pointed(Plate 40), but by 1640 they are more rounded on the lower side (Plate 26). At the same time there were Flemish laces for clerical use, that were used on the Mass vestments or the surplices. Plate 10 shows a seventeenth-century needlepoint lace, but the bobbin laces were just as much in demand then as they were later on in the eighteenth century.

Flemish ribbon lace

The 'Flemish ribbon lace' is quite individual and was a refinement of the linen type with a ribbon (name in lace work for the narrow band with an open-work edging on one side and a selvage on the other) forming a part of the design. The ribbon lies completely flat in these laces. The ornamental stitch is modestly worked in the lace in the form of small fillings of square meshes (fond à cinq trous). At the end of the seventeenth century these laces were developed into the beautiful laces with their graceful flowers, that were to become fashionable in the eighteenth century.

Brussels Lace

With the beginning of the eighteenth century the names Brussels and Brabants lace were often used instead of Flandres and this has created confusion. There is not enough historical evidence to be able to state accurately that this lace was made in Brussels. However, we can be certain of one piece of an earlier date, namely the remarkable foot cover, dated 1599 and given to Archduke Albert and his wife Isabella at their visit to the City of Brussels, on the occasion of their marriage and inauguration as Duke and Duchess of Brabant.
E. van Overloop says in his book *Matériaux pour servir à l'histoire de la dentelle en Belgique:*
    'This foot cover, 58 x 52 inches, is composed of squares, representing several royal personages, biblical stories and groups of the great Brussels 'processions'. Where the renaissance period was in every industrial art partial to the reproduction of everything that was Roman, it is

understandable that in this foot cover too the Roman kings and emperors and the prophetesses are not missing.'

He comes to the conclusion that 'to one standing on the threshold of the seventeenth century in the lace made in Brussels, there was already an outspoken preference for the figurative motif and the use of the relief, next to the floral motif'. This foot cover is in the collection of the Musées Royaux d'Art et d'Histoire in Brussels.

The Flandres laces made in the second half of the seventeenth century change from the loosely worked band-like flowers to more realistic leaves and flowers. In this lace bars with picots fill the background.

In the eighteenth century ribbon appears in Louis XIV laces, as a fine relief next to the prettier and richer motif stitches. Apart from that, the round mesh (as the Valenciennes ground) or the hexagonal (like the eighteenth century Mechlin ground) partly fills in the background of the Brussels laces. The most beautiful laces are made in this technique, and one cannot but admire the lappets of the caps, the cap-crowns, the jabot and the excellent flounce from the middle of the eighteenth century referred to earlier, which can be seen in the Rijksmuseum in Amsterdam. It is difficult to know which to admire more, the beautiful designs or the fine finish of the ornament or the ornamental stitches. It is a pity that we know nothing about the designers or workers. No designer's name is known, nor the name of the manufacturer who was responsible, and neither do we know anything about the women who spent so many hard hours working on the lace, although we do know that the workers sewing the *finest* thread often worked in damp cellars to prevent the thread becoming brittle.

In the first part of the eighteenth century lappets and crowns for caps, as well as pieces for dresses were made, that strangely enough did not have the bar ground from the seventeenth century nor the ground of meshes from the eighteenth century. These laces, worked in real Regency design are of a fantastic fineness and although the motif does not fit completely, the

62

design is beautiful. The later Louis XV laces are distinguished for Arabesques, richness of workmanship and elegance of designs.

During the Louis XVI period the high standard of the designers declines, the motif loses its brilliance and the hexagonal mesh has only sewn motifs on it and a row of ovals with ornamental stitches form the outer edging. The ornament is modest but unfortunately dull, which is not desirable in this art as the whiteness is only given life and colour with the correct grouping of light and shade towards which the endless variation of ornamental stitches also contributes. The final effect of a lace will show whether it was designed by a real artist for only he will have found the correct grouping of the stitches. Many Brussels laces made in the eighteenth century have this unbelievably beautiful flat division and have become real works of art. Fortunately as an example of these beautiful laces there is a broad flounce for priests clothing in the Boymans–Van Beuningen Museum in Rotterdam (Plate 42), while the Rijksmuseum also has a similar flounce in its collection.

The early eighteenth century design shown on Plate 42 is surprisingly peaceful with its symmetrical motifs placed alternately; the candle-crown and the cherubs on the altars show a particular elegance of composition and finish. These flounces were sometimes as wide as one yard in the eighteenth century.

In Belgian churches there are expensive eighteenth century flounces; exquisite pieces among the Benediction cloths, on which a miracle or some other religious or wordly event is pictured. Here the figurative takes an important place. When at the end of the eighteenth century the motif took up so little room that the lace was mainly background, this was worked in bands of about one inch in breadth and invisibly joined. The flowers and leaves were sewn on it, so that the appliqué on real background mesh had come into being. The Netherlands also own a Benediction cloth of this late

63

eighteenth century Brussels lace, in the collection De Monchy in the Boymans–Van Beuningen Museum. It is a picture of Christ being taken off the Cross (Plate 44). The figures are beautiful portrayed, partly in bobbin lace, partly in needlepoint lace. The floral ornament and the ornamental stitches in it have been bobbin made completely, just like the background called 'drochelground'. It is one of the finest cloths made in the latter part of the eighteenth century. These eighteenth century Brussels laces are sometimes called 'Vieux Bruxelles'.

In the beginning of the nineteenth century, the Brussels laces became popular again since Napoleon I and his Imperial household favoured Brussels lace, just as the Bourbons had done in the eighteenth century. Madame L. Paulis writes in the *Bulletin des Musées Royaux d'Art et d'Histoire* (September 1931):

'Of these early nineteenth century Brussels bobbin laces on fond drochel (possibly made of the Brussels patois 'thread') there are two panels in the Lescure Collection, reminding one of the school of David, and of superb technique. After the exhibition in Antwerp, the collection in the Koninklijke Musea voor Kunst en Geschiedenis, Brussels was enlarged with a spread of about 3 to 4 yards, completely worked in Brussels lace with unmistakable composition of post-Empire. Next to the great Empire rosette-flowers there are the twigs already pointing to the past glory of the First Empire. But except for that, the coats of arms and the crowns are the most interesting for they show that this great spread was made to order; the Russian coat of arms and the crowned C suggests that it was made for a Russian princess, most probably for Charlotte of Prussia, wife of the Russian heir to the throne, whom she married in 1817.'

For this spread the motif is completely made in bobbin lace. But there are also Brussels laces made in the eighteenth century, having a needlepoint lace motif or a partly needlepoint and partly bobbin lace one. These laces are often mentioned under the name Point d'Angleterre, but they were

44. *Benediction cloth, Brussels needlepoint and bobbin lace on a background of bobbin lace, so-called fond Drochel, representing the descent of Christ from the cross (late 18th century).*

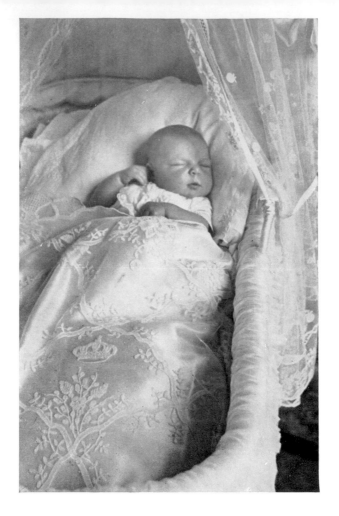

45. Appliqué of bobbin lace on tulle made by the Royal Netherland Lace School in 1909. 46. The ends or lappets of Brussels needlepoint lace on a bobbin lace background, so-called Point d'Angleterre (late 18th century).

47. Honiton lace cape — Mary Ireland Collection.

48. Carrickmacross cape, 19th Century
— Mary Ireland Collection.

49. Brussels lace shawl,
mid 19th Century
— Mary Ireland Collection.

definitely not made in England but in Belgium and were exported to England.

Appliqué de Bruxelles

After 1835 the making of genuine lace disappeared gradually as the machine-made tulle became popular. Next to the drochel, voilettes with the design of 1830—1840, appeared similar ones with a machined ground. It was very interesting to come upon two christening-veils some years ago, of exactly the same design, one with a needlepoint and the other a bobbin lace motif, applied on machine-made tulle and called Appliqué de Bruxelles. This Appliqué de Bruxelles assumed enormous proportions, since with this, lace suddenly became more within everyone's reach. The background was much cheaper, as the worker could make sixty meshes per minute, while the machine makes sixty thousand in the same time.

Duchesse, Rococo, Bruges fin or Flandres, Angleterre, Rosaline, Valenciennes de Brabant

The nineteenth century produced the Duchesse, the Rococo, the Bruges fin or Flandres, the Rosaline and the Valenciennes de Brabant. All of these are made with bobbins and although the method is the same they differ in design.

Duchesse has a rich, often overloaded floral motif; the Rococo a continuous principal line with small curls and flowers with three or five leaves, inspired by the seventeenth-century Venise à la Rose (also made in Italy); the Bruges fin or Flandres has an ever-twisting band in between which there

Pattern in Duchesse lace

are some ornamental stitches; the Rosaline is a finer lace in the type of the Rococo technique and can be distinguished by small reliefs of needlepoint lace in the centre of the round flowers. All these laces have 'bars' as a background. Only the Valenciennes de Brabant has a background of meshes resembling the Valenciennes ones and although the reproduction never shows this clearly, this kind of lace is not made in the Valenciennes but in the Brussels technique, worked in parts. All these laces are still made in Belgium.

Brabants, bobbin laces

In the eighteenth century laces made in the country were called Brabants laces. As contrasted with Brussels laces, they had a heavier cast-on design of larger motifs and no relief; they were worked with a thicker thread and mostly with less ornamental stitches. In the Collection de Monchy there is a flounce for clerical use (Plate 43), which is an exceptionally fine specimen of the Brabants laces, and the beautiful stitches in the ornament are worth closer inspection.

Holland

There were several lace schools in Holland in between the years 1850 and 1935, some of them supervised by the author of this book, and it was at one of these schools that Princess Juliana's cradle was made and given to the late Queen Wilhelmina by some of her subjects. The Queen wanted a cradle in the Louis XVI style and 34 workers were employed on it for 12,000 hours. Plate 45 shows a part of the spread, and the curtains and flounces with the orange design.

Since 1935, although repeated efforts have been made to keep it alive, the industry as such has not survived in Holland, but throughout the country bobbin lace is practised as a hobby, often with great skill.

English and Irish Laces

The best known laces of England are Honiton and Bucking-

Brabants bobbin lace

ham, though Mrs. Palliser lists the names of eleven English counties where lace was made. Ireland was celebrated for its Limerick and Carrickmacross laces and the crochet of Cork and Ross.

The earliest mention of lace-making in Honiton is by Westcote in 1620: 'Here is made an abundance of bone (i.e. bobbin) lace, a pretty toye now greatly in request' — while a later writer describes it as 'not expensive of bullion like other lace, costing nothing save a little thread descanted on by art and industry'.

All the finest thread used by English and Irish lace workers had to be bought from Antwerp — so also was the superfine net groundwork (costing £70 a pound if needle-made) which the Honiton workers imported — or smuggled — for the appliqué motifs in which they specialised; having adapted their designs and technique from Brussels workmanship — and which can be seen in the cape (Plate 47) which was a style fashionable in the 1850's.

It is difficult to trace the origin of Irish lace. In 1743 workhouse children in Dublin produced 'Bone lace to the value of £164.14.10d'. This was an imitation of Brussels lace. Carrickmacross lace was made there in 1820 and was constructed by the design being drawn on to fine cambric and applied to a net ground with point or tambour stitch, surplus cambric being cut away leaving the design sharp and clear as can be seen on Plate 48, which is an illustration of a lace cape of the 1860's made for a member of the Douglas family from a design on the Scottish 'heart' pattern.

Limerick lace was first made in 1829. It is composed entirely of tambour stitch worked on to net with a variety of thickness of cotton thread covering large floral designs which shows to great advantage on the shawls; both square and triangular, which were so popular during Queen Victoria's reign — as well as the narrower flounces and lace-by-the-yard used extensively at this time and into the Edwardian era. This particular stitch is a chain stitch done directly on the net work with a Tambour needle when the stretched net is held taut on a wooden framework. The stitch is of unknown origin, but came to Europe from the East and was used a thousand years ago in Persia, India, Turkey and China.

Illustrations

1 Maarten van Heemskerk: portrait of Anna Pietersd. Codde, dated 1529, Rijksmuseum, Amsterdam.
3 Property of the Royal Antiquarian Society, Rijksmuseum, Amsterdam.
4 T. Ravensteyn: Portrait of Beatrix van Sypesteyn (1593—1663), The De Sypesteyn Museum, Loosdrecht.
5 Giovanni Fasola (1528—1572): Venetian lady. Museum, Dresden.
6 Dirck Dircksz. Santvoort (1610—1680): child's portrait, Mrs. Kaars Sypesteyn-van der Feen de Lille, Krommenie, property of the De Dieu foundation.
7 Cornelis de Vos (1585—1651). Portrait of both his daughters. Collection de Sinebrychoff, Athenea Museum, Helsinki.
8 Q. G. van Brekelenkam (1620—1669): 'the Reader', Rijksmuscum.
9 Salomon Mesdach: Portrait of a man from the Boudaen Courten family, dated 1620, Rijksmuseum.
10 Bernardo Strozzi (1581—1644): Portrait of Bishop Aloise Grimani, Kress. Collection, National Gallery, Washington.
11 J. A. Lievens (1607—1674): Portrait of Engel de Ruyter, dated 1680, Rijksmuseum.
14 Portrait of H.M. the Queen Mother of the Netherlands.
15 J. v. d. Vaart: Portrait of Mary Stuart (1662—1695), wife of William III, Rijksmuseum.
17 Property of the Metropolitan Museum, New York.
18 N. P. Lepicie: 'The Astronomer', National Gallery, Washington.
19 J. M. Quinkhard (1688—1772): Portrait of Margaretha Trip, Rijksmuseum.
21 F. X. Winterhalter (1805—1873): Portrait of Marie Amélie, Queen of France, dated 1842, Museum of Versailles.
26 D. D. Santvoort (1610—1680): Portrait of Agatha Geelvink, dated 1640, Rijksmuseum.
27 C. J. van Geulen: Portrait of Ida 't Hooft, c. 1650, Museum Boymans-Van Beuningen, Rotterdam.
28 François Verwilt: Portrait of the son of Admiral van Nes, dated 1669, Rijksmuseum.
36 Copyright and owner Netherlands Open-Air Museum, Arnhem.
37 C. Kruseman (1797—1857): Portrait of Queen Anna Pavlovna as Princess of Orange, property of H.M. the Queen of the Netherlands.
39 F. J. de Goya (1746—1828): Portrait of Maria Louisa, Queen of Spain, Mellon Coll., National Gallery, Washington.
45 Property of H.M. Queen Juliana.

The laces shown under the numbers 16-22-23-32-33-34-35 and 41 are owned by the Rijksmuseum in Amsterdam.
Number 2-12-13-20-38-40-42-43 and 44 are owned by the Museum Boymans-Van Beuningen in Rotterdam.
Number 24-25-29-30-31 and 46 are privately owned.

Bibliography

Edith Appleton Standen, The Metropolitan Museum of Art. New York Bulletin Jan. 1958. The Grandeur of Lace.

Emile Bayard, L'art de reconnaître les dentelles, guipures etc. Paris 1914.

G. de Bever, La Dentelle. Bruxelles 1945.

Max. von Boehm, Die Mode, Menschen und Moden. (17th, 18th, 19th century. Six volumes.) München 1905.

A. Carlier de Lantsheere, Les dentelles à la main. Paris.

A. Carlier de Lantsheere, Trésor de l'art dentellier. Répertoire des dentelles à la main de tous les pays, depuis leur origine jusqu'à nos jours. Bruxelles & Paris 1922.

Mme. S. Davodoff, Russische Kant. Petersburg 1909 (in het Russisch verschenen).

Mme. G. Despierres, Histoire du Point d'Alençon depuis son origine, jusqu'à nos jours. Paris 1886.

L. Erkelens, Kant. Serie: Facetten der verzameling no. 5. Uitgave Rijksmuseum Amsterdam 1955.

Freiherr Alfred von Henneberg, Stil und Technik der alten Spitzen. Berlin 1931.

N. Hudson Moore, The Lace Book. London 1905.

L. Iklé und Dr Ad. Fäh, Die Sammlung Iklé. Zürich.

Mrs Neville Jackson and E. Jesurum, A History of Lace. London 1900.

Mme Laurence de Laprade, Le poinct de France et les Centres dentelliers au XVII et au XVIII siècle. Paris 1905.

E. Lefébure, Broderie et Dentelles. Paris 1887.

E. Lefébure, Les Points de France. Paris 1912.

Jhr E. van Loon, De Kantindustrie in Frankrijk en Italië. 's-Gravenhage 1904.

Mrs E. L. Lowes, Chats on old Lace & Needlework. London 1908, 1912, 1919.

Florence Lewis May, Hispanic Lace and Lace making. New-York 1939.

L. W. van der Meulen-Nulle, Kant. Amsterdam 1936.

L. W. van der Meulen-Nulle, De collectie kanten 'de Monchy': Bulletin Museum Boymans. Rotterdam april 1952. (Ook verschenen in The Illustrated London News May 1953).

W. H. de Monchy, Hoe een verzameling tot stand kwam. Bulletin Museum Boymans, Rotterdam april 1952.

Mej. Joh. W. A. Naber, Oude en Nieuwe Kantwerken. Haarlem 1903.

Mej. L. W. Nulle, Handleiding tot het vervaardigen van Duchessekant, 's-Gravenhage 1907, reprinted 1923. (L. W. van der Meulen-Nulle).

Eug. van Overloop, Matériaux pour servir à l'histoire de la dentelle en Belgique. Bruxelles 1902. Reprinted 1910.

Mrs Bury Palisser, History of Lace. London 1875, reprinted 1902.

Mme Bury Palisser, Histoire de la Dentelle. Paris 1890.

L. Paulis, Le Passé de la dentelle belge. Bruxelles.

L. Paulis, Les points à l'aiguille belges. Bruxelles 1947.

Elisa Ricci, Antiche Trine Italiane. Trine ad ago. Bergamo 1908.

Elisa Ricci, Trine a fuselli. Bergamo 1911.

Elis M. Rogge, Naaldkunst. Kantwerk. Handweven. Rotterdam 1923.

Marie Schuette, Alte Spitzen. (Nadel und Klöppelspitzen). Berlin 1914.

Marie Schuette, Alte Spitzen, aus Anlasz der Ausstellung im städtischen Kunstgewerbe-Museum zu Leipzig 1911. Leipzig 1912.

Spetsutskottet Vadshena Kant. Linkoping, Zweden.

Margaret Taylor Johnstone, Ragusa, the mystery spot in lace-history. New York 1930.

Meta Tønder, Tønder Kniplinger. Tönder 1954.

Pierre Verhaegen, Les industries à domicile en Belgique. Vol. IV. Vol. V. La dentelle et la broderie sur tulle. Bruxelles 1912.

Mr F. E. Vlielander Hein, Een opstel over kant. Tijdschrift 'Het Huis Oud en Nieuw'. Afl. 7. Juli 1911. Amsterdam.

Index

74

point d'esprit, 48, 49
„   en l'air, 13
Poll, 9
ponti fiaminghi, 43
ponti in aria fiaminghi, 43
Pourbus d. J., Frans —, 16
prohibitions, 19
„   in England, 22
punto à reticello, 30
„   in aere, 13, 31

Q

Quicherat, 15
quilles, 24
Quinkhard, J. M. —, 41, 55
Quintell, 13
Quintin, 11
Quinty, Pierre —, 13

R

raccord, point de —, 56
Raguse, point de —, 20
Ravensteyn, J. R. van —, 15
Récamier, Mme —, 25
Regency design, 62
„   period, 53
regulations, 19
Rembrandt, 19
reprise, point de —, 12, 47
reticella, 30, 45
reticello, punto à —, 30
Revolution, French —, 25, 52, 55
ribbon lace, Flemish —, 61
Ricci, Elisa —, 30, 31, 42, 59
rococo (lace), 65
Rococo (period), 53
Romana, Lucretia —, 43
Rosaline, 66
rose, English —, 45
rose, point de —, 29, 34
rose, Venise à la —, 34, 43
rosettes, 19
round ladies, collar, 22
round mesh, 52, 59, 62
ruches, 24
Rutland, Earl of —, 18
Ruyter, Engel de —, 21
„   , Michiel de —, 21

S

Santvoort, Dirck, Dircks. —, 17, 60
Savary, 53
scarves, 26
Schuette, Marie —, 59
Second Empire, 26, 55
Sera, Dominique de —, 13
Sévigné, Mme De —, 20
shawls, 26
Sickinghe, family —, 9
silver lace, 49, 50
smuggling, 23
Soissons, Countess of —, 20
Spanish Blonde, 56
spiders, 45, 53
square mesh, 50, 52, 59
Steenkerkentie, 21
Stuart collar, 16, 30
summerlace, 23
surplice, 28
Sypesteyn, Beatrix van —, 15

T

tabliers, 22, 24
Tagliente, Antonio —, 13
Talon, 35
Talon (de Beaufort), 35
Terborch, Gerard —, 21
thistle ornament, 45
tie ends, 23
toile claire, broderie sur —, 13
tournantes, 24
'trace', 30
triangular shawls, 26
Trip, Margaretha —, 41
Trolle lace, 50
Trousse, Mlle de la —, 20
tulle brodé, 26
tulle, machine-made —, 65
turn-down collar, 16, 18
Turner, Mrs. —, 17

V

Valenciennes, 23, 26, 27, 51
„   de Brabant, 65

76

Contents

78

Flemish needlepoint lace, seventeenth century — Brussels needle-point lace, eighteenth century — Brussels needlepoint lace, nine-teenth century

Italian bobbin laces — Gold and Silver laces — Flandreslace, Fond à cinq trous — Dutch lace — Flemish lace — Valenciennes lace — Binche lace — Mechlin lace — Chantilly lace — Blonde lace — Point de Paris — Lille lace — Cluny lace

Milanese lace — Milanese lace with string — Flandreslace — Flemish ribbon lace — Brussels lace — Appliqué de Bruxelles — Duchesse — Rococo — Bruges fin or Flandres — Angleterre — Rosaline — Valenciennes de Brabant — Brabants, bobbin laces — Holland — English and Irish laces